Common

an anthology of dynamic new working-class
monologues for actors

Published May 2022 by Team Angelica Publishing,
an imprint of Angelica Entertainments Ltd

Team Angelica Publishing
51 Coningham Road
London W12 8BS

TEAM
ANGELICA

www.teamangelica.com
A CIP catalogue record for this book is available from
the British Library

ISBN 978-1-9163561-5-3

LOTTERY FUNDED

Supported using public funding by
**ARTS COUNCIL
ENGLAND**

Disclaimer/Reclaimer

It's weird, after years of teaching so many actors to write business letters that avoid over-using the words 'I', 'Me' and 'My', if at all, to now be writing these forewords infested with I, I, I. But you know what? Even though this trilogy of books have been lovingly assembled as heartfelt offerings to the reader, and as showcases for the 200 brilliant writers who have poured themselves into every word, it's become so clear to me, me, me, that that this project, this labour of love, in which every word is written by someone else - is deeply personal.

I used to say, 'I don't want to be a black writer. Or a gay writer. Or a working class writer. I just want to be a writer.' Now I look back and think why not? Why did I think that being flavourless was radical? Why was I denying my herbs and spices? Why did I think my various perspectives and nuances were a distraction or deficit? Lots of writers think that way. Actors too. But who we are is not a limitation. It's a launch pad. It's an advantage. And lots of emerging creatives seem to be realising that fact more and more. Actors call out on social media for audition/showcase speeches that they can relate to. They write me emails asking for recommendations for working class monologues, LGBTQIA+ monologues, black, brown, Asian monologues. And more. I give them what I've written. But it's not enough. Try as I might, I haven't written enough or read enough to cover all the bases, to offer up all the nuances. What's needed is more writers.

And so we put out a call on social media for emerging writers (many of whom are actors themselves) who'd like to be mentored on how to write a great audition speech for queer actors, working class actors and/or underrepresented ethnicities... And so, six months and countless phone/WhatsApp feedback sessions later, we have these three books: *Fierce*, *Common* and *Lit*. Every speech is 3 minutes or less. Each one has its own attitude and vibe. Posh black voices, rural gay voices, educated council estate voices, stereotypes and anti-stereotypes and everything in between. Voices as various and complex as yours. This collection of speeches is for you. They're meant to be said, not read. Read 'em out loud. Whisper them. Shout them. Stretch them. Sing them. Bring them to life. Smash the audition. Stop the show. Be as gay or ethnic as you feel like being. Code switch. Nuance. Clarify. Enlighten. Challenge. Confuse. And if nothing between these covers does the business for you... write your own.

Rikki Beadle-Blair

Common Thoughts

Growing up on the council estates of South East London, my schoolmates and neighbours were my first actors. White, Black, Brown and Tan, British, Irish, Jamaican, Turkish, African, Pakistani, Indian, Chinese, Indonesian, all with *Only Fools and Horses* accents or middle-class wannabe variants and quick cockney wit. When I wasn't adapting my favourite movies, I'd write about them, trying to capture their humour, intelligence, fortitude. A huge inspiration was seeing Ken Loach's *Kes*, and reading the book (by Barry Hines) made me aware that we had stories to tell, rhythms to honour and complexities to reveal. My friends' voices have never left me, they're here all the time, watching over my shoulder, urging me to write us all down. To do us justice. And they were there with me when we held the first Zoom workshop with the writers of this book. And the months of reading, note-sharing via WhatsApp, re-reading, debating, suggesting, coaxing, encouraging, fanboying with each writer – reminding to respect them and their influences and inspirations in the same way. After all, they carry their own voices with them too. And the results are thrilling. Moving. Magical. I am humbled by the range of working class experiences from across our society. I've learned so much. And I'm still learning. This is a book by 70 of my teachers, packed with working class wit, grace, tenderness, cheekiness, pain, despair, passion and resilience. And I'm proud to say, they have done their people justice.

Rikki

Table of Contents

A Crack Commandment to Follow by Alfie Neill 1

A Sheep in Wolf's Clothing by Sam Purkis 4

A Wank a Day Keeps the Bad News at Bay by Sam Purkis.............. 7

Barnaby by Hosanna Johnson... 9

Be Careful Who You Call An Essex Girl by Georgia Daniels 11

Better Than Me by Katie Hitchcock.. 14

Blub by Katie Hitchcock 16

Bluebells by Marika Mckennell 18

Boarding School Type Wanker by Siôn Rhys 21

Bottoms Up by Reuben Massiah 23

Breathe/Anadla Gan by Mali O'Donnell 26

Bricking It by Saffia Kavaz 35

Careers Day by Eloise Kay 38

Caviar by Sam Butters.. 41

Checking Out Lucy by Sam Harry MacGregor 44

Checkout by Ellen Lilley.. 47

Coming Out by Paul Culshaw 50

COONCIL (KID) by Amber Sinclair-Case 53

Date Night by Jordan John.. 56

Description by Winnie Imara... 59

Devil by Vanessa Schofield... 62

Dickhead by Jane Ryan... 64

Dog Mum by Nieve Hearity 67

Estate of Mind by Karen Whyte 70

Eyes Up by Gail Egbeson 74

Flying Too Close to The Son by Sam Purkis 77

Free School Meal by Dominic Holmes 81

Gateway to the Soul by Connor Allen 84

Gluten Free by Adil Hassan 87

Growing Out by Rachelle Grubb 90

Healthy Heart by Nicole Joseph 93

I Saw a Boy Hug His Dad by Amin Ali 95

Kev by Hannah Tarrington 97

Kneel by Warren Mendy 100

Lazy by Alistair Wilkinson... 102

Let this be beautiful by Tom Colgan... 105

Lobster by Benjamin Salmon.. 108

Lost Boy by Aimee Pollock 111

Love Language by Lauren Greer 114

Love Me Or Die by Josie White.. 117

Ninety-Six by Christie Reynolds.. 119

Not Compatible With Life by Nieve Hearity 121

Our Last Adventure by Charis McRoberts 124

Pavement Boss Man by Aoife Smyth 126

Peace in this hoos by Sarah Ord.. 129

Proud by Lekhani Chirwa 132

Puppy Pound by Sam Purkis... 135

Radical Temptation by James G. Nunn 138

Rouge by Rachelle Coffie 140

Rough on Smooth by Sam Purkis 143

RUN DOG BARK by Alexander Da Fonseca.................................. 145

Seahorse by Sarah Ord... 148

Sent to Cov by Tom Wright 151

SH*T by Becky Lennon 154

Shoot Your Load and Go by Vicky Wild 157

Split the Bill by Tricia Wey.. 160

Tactics by Sam Butters.. 164

The Look by Sam Liu... 167

The Offer by Daniel Reid-Walters 171

The Spider by Aaron Douglas 174

The Unravelling of Linus Wong by Stephen Hoo 176

Their Life My Lie by Kadiesha Belgrave 179

Two Cities by Paul Bradshaw 182

Uniform by Barbara Williams.. 184

Voice by Sam Purkis 187

Wee Audrey and the Lockjaw Monster by Lynne Jefferies 190

When the Fun Stops by Shakira Newton..................................... 192

Wrecked by Timotei Cobeanu... 195

You and Me, Stinky-Arse by Deanna Arthur 197

A Crack Commandment to Follow
by Alfie Neill

Interview room, London police station. RICK has been in a police cell all night. He's briefing an on-call community solicitor.

Rick   I told my mum I don't need a solicitor, I've done nothing wrong, but she was having none of it. But – yeah, all I hear is: Bang! Bang! Bang! It woke me up, shit scared. This is at like one in the morning. I go to the spy hole. Can't see a thing – Bang! Again. I go to the kitchen window and I see it's my neighbour, it's Des. He's a good man but he gets into a lot of trouble. These boys are outside waiting for him. Des is pleading with them:

'Oi, come on boys! Please!'

'We ain't done nothing to you!'

So I pull my phone out and start filming it.
More and more people are waking up, lights in the block are flickering on. All the nosey neighbours are out.

All of a sudden I see Des make a run for it, and they chase him to the ground. 'You fucking crackhead! Don't ever come to us again. You understand?'
Then heads are colliding. Blood is flying. Legs are kicking endlessly in the air.

Neighbours sharing screams. Shouting for them to get off him. So I put on my dressing gown, init. Slide into my sliders, I'm ready to go out there!

I've got down there now and the fucking feds have turned up.

I'm telling them Des is badly hurt. He's trying to get up but he's in pain. Of course the officers rush in – and just inflict more pain – restrain – contain. Hold down his squashed soul out of their disdain.

Anyway, we've crowded around in our pyjamas, phones out, all recording this injustice that is swelling. I can still hear him asking them to get off. They make a barrier around him so we can't see anything. I want to just push through but I remembered this composure workshop at the youth centre, before they closed. How to disarm a situation. So I go up to the pig and I ask the simple question, 'Can you state the reason for this man's arrest?'

This officer looks at me in the disbelief that I dare question him. Well, I held my phone so tight and made sure to catch everything!

Look where it's gotten me. A charge of disorderly conduct cos I obstructed their duty.

A duty to cause suffering.

All I can say is the video speaks for itself.
I mean, yeah, we know he's a junkie, but do you

know what? The man needs help, he doesn't need to be handcuffed.

But I guess we'll get up tomorrow morning and by night the sirens will hound again and the shouting of these lost souls will get louder.

They'll leave it to us, the 'community', to 'report it' because we need to look out for each other, but I think we need to stop looking out and start looking within.

Beat.

Is that enough for you?

A Sheep in Wolf's Clothing
by Sam Purkis

ALBY has approached a group of men standing in an alleyway. He feels the sharp object in his pocket and briefly flashes the handle. He's trying not to use it, so he says something instead.

Alby   A few years ago this was the part where I'm meant to hand you my phone and any cash in my pocket, wonnit? I can't believe I'm talking to you. I'm really learning to communicate at the moment. Use your words, you know? That's what my boyfriend tells me. To be honest mate, I thought the next time we saw each other I was going to stab holes in you until you looked like an inverted hedgehog. Right then. Well for starters I've got no cash and I've got an iPhone 4 so you'll be lucky to get fuck all for that. I've got to say as well, I don't think you boys are worth giving anything to. You've lost your touch or maybe now I'm thinking you never had it. I don't buy it, I just don't buy this.

See the thing is, lads – especially you, Robin of Cocksley and your little band of merry cunts – you think you know real violence, that's your first mistake.

Secondly, you see that weed you're smoking? That's mine. Those glacier-like shining nugs were grown with these hands, so obviously I don't come out unarmed or without people in that next garden who have more firepower than Elon Musk.

What are we on... Three? Still calm, aren't we? The third is that you think going to the gym to build your push up bra holders, working in the same fucking insurance firms as your dad's as you watch him hanging out his secretary whilst your mum's cooking unseasoned shepherd's pie and snorting some coke off the toilet seat, means you're living an existence comparable to being animal. It's false. Granted it's not your fault middle class Britain has taught you that getting a sleeve which looks like you've fisted the Dulux paint dog and starting a drug habit is a primal life experience. Although I've got to say you, Pat Butcher, at least you went the extra mile of bollocks and got an earring. Fuck me you're punchable. It lives inside some of us, it's like a fucking virus, a venom that you can feel in your head all day. You can feel it flood your chest and squeeze it until you pant like a dog in that festival, waiting to chomp the fucker trying to skin it. You feel it creep its way up your neck, trying to tear the veins out. It hits the brain and you can't see or feel anything apart from doing some serious fucking damage. It stops being personal, it's fucking animal. It's natural, mate, and this ain't your fucking ecosystem, lads.

Obviously your crops are now mine. You can put

them in the van. They've grown from last time you left your bathroom window open. Lots of leftover soil.

This isn't enough. I'm not satisfied with this ending. Sorry, babe. I've talked even though you're giving me nothing. I didn't deserve any of that. I've given you a few moments of peace, which is a few fucking more than you ever gave me. I think, Robin, I'll put my knife in your jaw and turn you into a Pez dispenser. Tweedle Dee, I'm gonna see if I can stamp your shins into a right angle. Tweedle Cunt, I'll flush you with Domestos and take bets on which end of you gives out first. Don't worry, I'm not a monster, they're just words – but I will take the earlobes off of one of you. I think that's fair. Would you like a minute to discuss? Right. We both know it's got to be you, Patty boy.

Well done mate, you're finally gonna get a taste of what you've been pretending to drink.

I am fucking riddled with violence. You want it, you search it out, you idolise it – which shows me you're nothing, you're frauds, you're fucking prey to me. So pray to me before I shed my human skin.

A Wank a Day Keeps the Bad News at Bay
by Sam Purkis

Tommy   I would just like to address the video that was released on Twitter and other socials last night. I know that many of my fanbase feel let down by my behaviour.

Yes, that was me on the tape. Yes, that was my penis. So I'd like to address my girlfriend who has always supported me, my family, my fans and the international media... and apologise to no one whatsoever.

Simple fact is, I was having a good, ol' fashioned, private, consensual as always, gorgeous, muscular, sensual, primal, massaging, breathy, full bodied, leg aching, toe curling, ankle stretching, nirvana inducing wank. A full pint hand shandy. A one-man explosive stream of liquid bliss from my joyful love-cannon.

I don't usually call it that. But maybe from now on I will.

I feel compelled to add, it was fucking well worth it. I'm worth it. I'd recommend coconut oil. Spa like. Almost shamelessly indulgent. Grab your balls. Do it properly. Spoil yourself.

I know about all the jokes speculating what I was watching. Was it porn? I'd gone beyond that. That's

just phase one wanking. Then it's music. I trans-
cended that night – ballet. Always wanted to do
that – so beautiful, elegant: the human peaking:
chiselled bodies, the gentleness and drama of the
music; they're so fucking fit in every sense, mixing
art and orgasm. Like art, orgasms are great alone or
with company. A larger number of people creates
more atmosphere, more to play with, heightened
communal bliss, a chorus of ecstasy – but with more
people come more aromas, smells, stenches. Inhale
'em all.

Life is filled with people failing to communicate and
having a shit time because no one allows themselves to find out what they want – billions of
frustrated fuckers frozen in self-loathing, and loath-
ing the world for the shame they feel, and trying to
make you and me feel guilty for it.

Let the world know what you like, what you want.
When one plant dares to dart at the sun and bloom
it fertilises and enriches everything around it.
Metaphorical fertilisation, you dirty bastards. Forget
protection, go solo bareback an' let your creative
juices flow. No pulling out. I think I'll try an opera
next, cum along to an aria. If I practice hard enough,
who knows? I might hit a low note or two.

Barnaby
by Hosanna Johnson

Alex   Remember three months ago when I said I wanted driving lessons for my twenty-first? Begged you for them. Remember when I said that I didn't want anything else in the world? Then you tried to save up for them. Well, I've changed my mind and I don't want lessons anymore. I want nothing to do with cars.

I bought a bicycle last week, not expensive or anything. It's a dirty red road bike. It looks like it could be vintage, but it's just old. Bit like you. Joking of course. You are vintage, classic... like a fine cheese.

Bikes are better, you know, for the environment and for the wallet and for the fun factor. I ride loads at night because I've been having trouble sleeping. Instead of going to bed, I get on Barnaby at one or two in the morning and cycle into the night. I don't even know where I'm going. Once I found an Ikea that I thought was our Ikea, but it wasn't, it was the Tottenham one! Ikea has an apocalyptic atmosphere at four a.m. I might try cycling to Brighton and back. Google maps has a good route. It's ambitious, but it would be kinda thrilling to see an empty beach. That's what I love about cycling. I feel alone and in control. It's ultimate freedom – just me, Barnaby and the streetlights, no thoughts or anything. It can be dangerous, but I wouldn't want you to worry about me. If anything, it's making me healthier. With that in mind —

I bought you a bike too. Surprise! I thought Barbara, maybe? Or Bradley — it's up to you. Of course you'll have to fully recover before we can go out riding together, but we can take it slow. If your stroke has taught me anything it's that we need to get your blood flowing, heart pumping, lungs inhaling, legs rotating and butt gyrating. That's another thing about cars I don't like. You just sit in them and do nothing.

I wanted to move out. Sorry, but I wanted to get far away from our flat and live somewhere totally different. Now I'd rather have Barnaby because I quite like staying close, you know? Cars just create more distance.

You worked hard to try and afford lessons for my birthday, I'm not ungrateful. It's just, now it's my turn to work hard for you. Buy Barbaras and Barnabys for us. So maybe on my birthday we can go for a gentle ride together. Or maybe we'll start with a walk? Spend some time with each other, talk. That's what I'd want. More than anything.

Be Careful Who You Call An Essex Girl
by Georgia Daniels

LEANNE, 24, Essex.

Leanne I'm sorry, I know I've had my time slot, but I had to come back in to get this off my chest so it doesn't burden the rest of my day 'cause this isn't fair. You haven't been fair.

I saw the way you were looking at my CV and you know what, this time it hurt. Now, I've got resilient skin as thick as a fucking rhino, but you cannot say I don't tick every box for this role, because I do. That is why I applied. This job is perfect for me and I am perfect for this job. But because my address says Essex I have to deal with the backlash of lazy brain-washed minds.

Sorry, you can't deny it. The first thing you said to me in my interview was, 'Oh... you're an Essex Girl'... with a smile even more fake than your full set of veneers – no offence, mine too, yours are excellent by the way – triggering my own false smile while I sat dying in that degrading and uncomfortable set-too-low spinning chair.

Yes, I'm an Essex girl, born and bred and proud of it. But as soon as someone reads those two words, it's like all my achievements turn invisible. And that's so normal you probably never even noticed yourself

11

thinking it, but I did and that shit cuts deep, ya know? People mocking the way I talk, assuming all the oldest stereotypes in the book, locking me away in the TOWIE category and chucking away the key.

Pulls out mobile phone and reads from it.

'Essex Girl - a young working-class woman from the Essex area, typically considered as being unintelligent, materialistic, devoid of taste, and sexually promiscuous'. That is in the fucking *Oxford English Dictionary*. A whole society of women slung together in a sentence.

That's what was in your mind when you saw my CM19 postcode. That's how you decided to see me all through our 15 minutes no matter what I said or thought or showed you.

I really wanted this job. Researched. Studied. I know why the turnover for this job is so rapid, and I could see exactly why the previous candidates for this job haven't worked out. 'Cause you always go for the same sort of person, and they don't connect with the demographic you're trying to sell to. Well I do, so I made every effort possible to be my best and most genuine self. And instead of using your position and education to see and hear me, you made your mind up in advance to barely glance at me and send me back to Harlow with my tail between my legs.

There's loads of types of intelligence in this world, and you know what? 'Essex Girl' is one of them. Yeah, we can be a lot of things. Some of us have dodgy taste. Some of us are sexually promiscuous. So what? So's the royal family. Meanwhile, our working-class parents have taught us how to work hard and work our way up. I am educated. I am fiercely loyal. I am hard-working. I am sociable. I am a team player and I am 100% qualified for this position. And if you miss out on me, I feel sorry for you. 'Cause you need me.

You need an Essex Girl.

Better Than Me
by Katie Hitchcock

Gabby What the fuck are you laughing at? Don't go all
quiet now. Why are you laughing at me, Lauren?
Stood there with your gang of so-called mates and
your sad little prefect badge, thinking you're –
what? *Better* than me?

Oh okay, I get it. Just cos your mum is a teacher
and shops at M&S and cooks you gourmet fucking
stir-fried packed lunches while I bring in Nutella
sandwiches and go home to eat frozen pizzas or
whatever from Iceland. Waltzing around in your
brand new Clark's brogues thinking you're God's
precious gift with his holy light shining out of your
arse.

But d'ya know what? I'm proud of what I've got and
what I eat. Cos my mum works for every bit of it. In
the corner shop – the one down Giddon Road?
Yeah. You wouldn't know that cos you wouldn't be
seen dead stepping foot in there cos you think it's
too chavvy. And anyway your mum and dad don't
let you walk down that street cos it's full of 'scum'
and they're nice polite middle-class Tory racists. My
mum works there, 13 hour shifts five times a week,
stocking shelves pissed out of her fucking brain, two
bottles of wine and a bottle of vodka down and you
know what, not a fucking soul can tell that she has

five kids including me at home and a husband who's a useless cunt with a steroid addiction.

And now you're probably thinking that *does* mean you're better than me. That I'm lower than fucking low, when actually it makes *me* better than *you*. Because I don't rely on Mummy and Daddy to wipe my fucking arse. I go home, I look after my Mum whilst she's chucking her guts up at two in the morning. I go home, I take care of my siblings and parents and I fucking get on with it.

See Lauren, the most pathetic thing is, I actually used to idolise you. I wanted to be you *so* bad in every way. I used to go home after school, look at my mum, my dad, my shitty little house and think, 'Please God, let me wake up as Lauren.' Because you get everything so, so easy. Your big group of mates, your fancy lunches, your functioning family who actually give a shit about you. You don't have to worry about a thing. But actually, now, I've realised that I don't. I don't want to be anything like you. Because you and your 'mates' are a bunch of stuck up twats and I couldn't think of anything worse than having to spend all my time licking your arse so I can look 'cool'.

So actually, no, Princess Lauren, you're not better than me, you're not even close. And you, your mum, your dad and your mates can all go and fuck yourselves.

Blub
by Katie Hitchcock

Ellie   Do you think I'm fat? And don't just say no to be nice.

Every time I look in the mirror all I can see is this big lump of blub above, like, my vagina. And I'm like, that seriously cannot just be my womb. Like on Twitter the other day someone tweeted that apparently women shouldn't feel bad about having a bulgy stomach because that is literally our ovaries? But then I saw someone reply, 'That's fuckin bollocks coz how come some women have flat stomachs then?' So... I guess that's not true.

But then I do wonder, would my head even suit like, Kendall Jenner's body? Because the fact is I do have quite a large head, whatever weight I get to. Like, I could be five stone and anorexic and still have a head like Shrek. I think I'd look like one of those pencils with the fuck off massive ball rubber things on the end. My mum has a fat head too. I think it must be genetics.

It does keep me warmer in the winter though. Acts as an extra layer. Well, that's what my mum says anyway. Sometimes I look at it and I just think... is it really that bad? Having a little bit of a belly? Cos it doesn't mean I'm unhealthy or anything. Although obviously I don't exercise or anything like that, but, I dunno. Sometimes I just think that actually, it makes me look quite like… cute? You know because like, you never see a skinny teddy bear? They're always a little bit chubby and tatty which makes you want to squeeze them and hug them, and loads of people sleep with teddy bears so… Actually, maybe people secretly want to sleep with me too? Not sexually. Well, maybe sexually. To be fair, I wouldn't mind either way.

I guess I'd like to just be able to walk around in my underwear without feeling ashamed because of how I look. Or wear a bikini to the beach without worrying that people are looking at me and thinking I'm fat or gross or whatever. Like I'd be better if I was skinnier.

I don't know. Maybe I should just stop eating so many mozzarella dippers. Or actually run instead of just thinking about it.

What do you think?

Jessie? Oi! Jessie man, will you get off your fucking phone!

Bluebells
by Marika Mckennell

LOLITA, 15 years old.

Lolita   I didn't know she was lying.

We have the bag, she said get off the train, so we did. Before you say, 'Would you follow her if she jumped off a bridge?' or some cliché shit like that, the answer is yes. I would jump off a bridge. Or do anything for her, coz that's ride or die, alright?

We get out of the station, and she says we're meeting T in another village. I felt like we were Britain's Most Wanted the way people were watching us. Mind you I'm used to it. She loves dragging me to posh places, hipster coffee shops 'n' shit. I tried to tell her some places ain't for us, like this town. But she's been OT before, she knows where to go.

We get on a bus, which only comes once an hour, and they don't take Oyster. A women with too much skin and a slobbering dog wants convo. She says, 'You simply must see the bluebells,' and Janie strokes her fat, black dog and I feel like everyone on the bus is staring at me. The women's banging on about ancient trees, but I don't know what they are and Janie don't either, so we jump off.

Outside the Horse and Groom pub there's bikes, loads of them, just sitting there. Maybe they're like

Jump bikes? If they're not Jump bikes people are hella trusting here. Must be a country thing. Imagine living somewhere you don't have to lock your bike? True say Janie doesn't have to. No one's gonna jack her bike coz everyone knows she's T's girl.

We borrow one bike, promising each other we'll bring it back. We're flying down this country path. The air is so fresh. I'm gulping it down like it's Rio Tropical or something. It's the best air I've ever smelt, and I've forgotten all about what we came for, because it's just me and her and this bike and this fresh air.

The path starts to turn into trees, bare trees. Everywhere you look are these massive things, like tower blocks but living and growing. I didn't know trees could get that big. It's all green at the top, and then on the bottom there's this colour. Some mad colour. I've never seen anything like it. Purplish and blue, it's like a carpet of flowers. It looks like fairyland. The way the light is shining though the leaves onto the petals, they look like fairy hats, or upsidedown bells. I have never in my life seen anything like that.

I remember we played a game. Something we haven't done since we were in primary. She wanted to pretend to be a princess and I was like fuck that coz everyone knows it's sexist and unrealistic. But we played it anyway. Coz Janie wanted to. Running around in the flowers making the belly of a huge hollow tree a castle and our home. It was all ours. The whole place was ours.

Then the best bit happened. This animal. I don't know what it's called, I completely forgot its name. Janie says it's a goat, but I know that ain't right. It's got these big black eyes and they're staring right at us. Janie takes my hand and I feel this flash of electricity shoot right up my arm. And it's like it's looking at us and into us, and I just feel like everything is gonna be okay.

Then suddenly the animal legs it and the magic stops.

I tell her we have to find T, coz we came here for a reason. I told her you'll murder us if we don't get this bag to you. Then she tells me she made it up. She says you're waiting in another town. She's running away.

Boarding School Type Wanker
by Siôn Rhys

Adam   What have you done with my mate? Because this dickhead stood in front of me, he ain't the guy I grew up with. What happened to the guy who didn't give a shit, the guy who would look at who you are now and laugh? Now you're just some prim and proper Cambridge boy, are ya? Just spend your time attending fancy dinners where they call you Geoffrey to make you sound all proper, like you're one of them. Is that what they do to you, strip you of all the things that make you vaguely likeable? Turn you into some empty talking head that spouts nothing but facts and figures and philosophical bullcrap? Is it them that's made you into this boarding school type wanker? Or did you do this to yourself? Are you that ashamed of us, of me, your friends, your family, this town? Are we that far beneath you now? Well, I'm so sorry that you've been forced against your will to come back here for the summer and pretend that you're happy to be around us. It's obvious that you'd rather be back at college with your fellow 'intellectuals' instead of being stuck here in the asshole of civilisation with those you deem inferior, you know, the losers and fuckups who raised you, who you were brought up alongside, who made you the person who got where you are today. But bollocks to all that, just throw them by the wayside why don't you, because it's not

worth anything is it? It's not like we're human fucking beings who actually genuinely give a shit about
you. Well, sorry, 'Geoffrey'. Sorry that I can't be
what you require from a mate anymore. I'm sorry
I'm no longer worthy of your time. And believe it or
not, deep down I'm happy for you that you've
moved on to where you want to be, but this town,
these people, they're all I have. And I won't let you
talk about it in front of us as if it's some shithole! So
just fuck off back to Cambridge.

But before you go, I'll tell you one last thing for
nothing. They'll never see you as their equal. It
won't matter what you do, you can ace every exam,
learn everything there is to learn, you could even
start shopping at fucking Waitrose and get a loyalty
card, but no matter how hard you try to mask the
scent of where you grew up, to them you'll always
stink of Lidl. Deny it all you want, you'll always be
one of us.

Bottoms Up
by Reuben Massiah

CAMERON sits across from Baz and Collin at the pub close to work.

Cameron If I could change one thing at the office Collin, it would probably be... you.

I'm not sure how many times I need to tell you but I'm NOT Tim. I don't have dreadlocks, I don't have a beard and I don't coat my shirts in cheap Tesco brand Lynx! Every so often you ask me how Yolanda and Grace are, forgetting that they are Tim's kids. It's not that hard to TELL US APART! Oh, shut up Baz! You're the one who insisted on me drinking six shots the moment we got here to 'catch up' with you guys. Plus we're using Collin's open door chat policy right now. What's *said* in the circle, *stays* in the circle.

Have you ever wondered why Tim hasn't told you to piss off every time you ask him if he can rap or whether he can do a Jamaican accent? 'Cause when Tim's not complaining about his bratty, snotty kids he's yapping about you helping him up the career ladder. Yeah yeah yeah, every team meeting you go on and on about mentoring new leaders in the company, but let's face it, YOU are just one GIGANTIC equal opportunity bullshitter, aren't you?

And even me. You know I used to believe you actually gave a shit. Used to hang on your every piece of advice. Used to read any articles you sent. Used to spend half of my paycheck on leadership management books. Used to explain away the odd racist comment here and there cuz I thought, 'Nah, Collin's got my back. I work ten times harder than any of these clowns. It'll all pay off.' And did it? Did it my arse.

The truth is that us first-in last-out mugs have totally missed the most important thing on the list, which is getting drinks with Collin and 'the guys' every Friday before staggering home broke and rat-arsed like poor sad Baz here. All week long you snigger and laugh about the stupid things Baz did at Friday night drinks. But whenever I ask what happened, you always say, 'Oh you'd have to be there to understand,' as if me and Tim couldn't wrap our highly educated brains around Baz making a fool of himself crawling up your backside. But it's clear as day, it works! If you're not in boss-man Collin's drinking club, you are out. You don't actually think anybody wants to spend their Friday night getting cirrhosis of the liver with a scruffy bully, do you? They drink to get your attention, mate, your time and focus, and your recommendations for promotions. And you know it and you take advantage of it, cause it's all you have. Maybe if I had 'joined in' I'd have got the assistant IT manager promotion and I'd

be as desperate and low-key suicidal inside as Baz.
But I suppose it's what's on the outside that counts
right?

Toasting.

Bottoms up, arse-lickers!

Drinks.

You know what, you're right, Baz! This is a damn
good laugh and a wicked night out! I should definitely come to Work Drinks Fridays more often.
Your round, boss-man!

Breathe/Anadla gan
by Mali O'Donnell

ANNES, a young woman in her 20s.

Annes   Shhh, shhh, it's okay, it's fine. It's all going to be okay.

Isaac?
Can you hear me?

Look at you.
You have no idea.
Golden world.
You had that.
You had.

One from Cyncoed,
One from Cowbridge
One from Llantwit.
A pick and mix of all the poshest.
The privilege.
Such a golden world.
Full of hope and endless support.
You had that.
You had them.
All three of them.
You was their little experiment – bit of rough,
macho man – that they could talk to all their posh
friends about.
Laughing at you

Bettering yourself just by being with them.

The arrogance.

I never done that to you.

I never made you feel small.

Less than what you was.

I sat here while you made me look like a dickhead.

Shhh, shhh, it's okay, it's fine. It's all going to be
okay.

I wanted to be one of them posh girls who lived in
an incredible house with massive gardens and own
a horse.

I'd name mine Alan

Because I thought that was funny. Like who has a
horse named Alan?

Anyways.

We'd go down the beach and then to Porthkerry
and then gallop home.

Me and Alan like fucking Aslan and Lucy from
Narnia. Joined at the hip.

I didn't get Alan.

Never rode a horse.

I got Isaac.

Not a horse.

Joined at the hip but not in the Aslan and Lucy
way.

I wonder at what age you lose that.

Lucy and Aslan.

That childlike awe of the world.
That innocence.

You wouldn't know, would you?
Isaac?

Silent now.
Finally.
Took your time
Telling me to leave
to give up,
didn't fuck hard enough,
fast enough,
pretty enough.
That I wasn't enough.
Enough.
Slap
Enough.
I'd had enough.
I told you.
I was done.
But you never listened. Always came back wanting
more, stealing more, raging more.
And then so did I.
Kick.
Enough.
Kick.
Enough.
Breathe.
Not so loud now. Not so proud now. I didn't mean

to go that far.

Shhh, shhh, it's okay, it's fine. It's all going to be okay.

Floor – carpet, Walls – chips and curry sauce,
Windows – white, Sky – blue skies
Mouth – smile
If you could read my mind you would not be smiling.

Oh no.

It's all going to be okay.
I don't think it is.
Taste... Blood.
Iron... Like when you suck on a penny.
My mouth,
His mouth
Shit.
Are you hurt?
Did I do that?
Kick.
Enough.
Kick.
No, no you have to be quiet. Shush please. No one can know. Please.
QUIET.

Pause.

Smell... Varnish, like the old kind that you stole to put on your school shoes, from your nan's cupboard under the sink.
Breathe.

Breathes in.

Panics.

Are you breathing?
Please Isaac.
Please breathe.

WELSH VERSION

Anadla gan
Mali O'Donnell

ANNES – merch yn ei 20au

Shhhh, shhh mae'n iawn, mae'n iawn mae popeth y n mynd i fod yn iawn.

Issac?
Ti'n gallu clywed fi?

Edrycha arnat ti,
S'dim cliw gyda thi .
Byd o Aur
Yn berchen i ti.

Roedd gennyt ti

Un o Gyncoed,
Un o'r Bontfaen,
Un o Lantwit,
Pic and mix o'r cyfoethog.
Y freintiedig.
Byd o Aur,
Llawn gobaith a chefnogaeth ddiddiwedd.
Yn berchen i ti,
Roedd gennyt ti,
Gefaist ti'r tri.
Ti oedd ei arbrawf – ei darn garw, ei macho man-
 yr un roedden nhw yn gallu siarad â'i ffrindiau amd
ano.
Yn chwerthin arnat,
Yn gwella dy hun 'mond gan fod o'i chwmpas.
Yr haerllugrwydd.
Nes i byth 'na i ti,
Byth di 'neud i ti deimlo'n fach
Yn llai nag oeddet
Nes i eistedd yma tra bod ti yn 'neud i mi edrych fel
dickhead.
Roeddwn i eisiau bod yn un o'r merched posh oedd
yn byw mewn tai anghredadwy gyda gerddi masif'
a cheffylau.
Byddwn un i o'r enw Alan.
Achos o'n ni'n meddwl tase fe'n ddoniol. Pwy sy gyd
a cheffyl o'r enw Alan?
Beth bynnag,

Byddwn ni'n mynd lawr i'r traeth, yna i Borthceri ac wedyn nôl gartref.

Fi ac Alan, fel fucking Aslan a Lucy o Narnia.

Di ymuno wrth y glun.

Ges i byth Alan.

Bydd di farchog ceffyl.

Ges i Isaac.

Dim ceffyl.

Di ymuno wrth y glun, ond nid yn yr un ffordd.

Tybed pryd chi'n colli hwnna.

Lucy ag Aslan

Parchedig ofn y byd.

Y diniweidrwydd.

Bydda ti ddim yn gwybod, byddet ti?

Isaac?

Tawelwch

Distaw nawr.

O'r diwedd

Cymer dy amser.

Nes ti dweud wrtha'i adael

I roi'r gorau iddi

Ddim yn fuck digon caled,

Digon cyflym

Digon pert

Ddim yn ddigon.

Digon

Slap

Digon.

Ges i ddigon

Nes i ddweud wrthyt ti
Ges i ddigon.
Nes ti byth gwrando. Wastad yn dod 'nôl, yn eisiau
mwy, dwyn mwy, yn cynddeiriogi mwy.
Ac wedyn nes i
Cic
Digon
Cic
Digon
Anadla
Ddim mor gryf nawr. Ddim mor falch nawr. Doeddw
n i ddim am fynd mor bell â hynny.

Shhhh, shhh mae'n iawn, mae'n iawn mae popeth y
n mynd i fod yn iawn.

Lawr – carped, waliau – sglods a
saws cyri, ffenestri – gwyn, awyr – awyr las
Ceg – gwên
Os gallet ti ddarllen fy meddwl tase ti ddim yn chwe
rthin.
O Na.
Mae popeth yn mynd i fod yn iawn.
Sai'n credu bod hi
Blas – gwaed
Haearn .. fel sugno ar geiniog
Fy ngheg
Ei geg
Shit
Wyt ti wedi brifo?

Nes i dy frifo ti?
Cic
Digon
Cic
Na, na mae'n rhaid i ti fod yn dawel. Shush plîs.
Does neb yn gallu gwybod. Plîs.
TAWELWCH.

Saib.

Arogl … farnais, fel yr un hen roeddet ti yn dwyn o
dan y sinc yn dŷ nain, i roi ar esgidiau ysgol.
Anadla

Mae'n Anadlu.

Wyt ti'n anadlu?
Plîs Isaac.
Plîs anadla.

BRICKING IT
by Saffia Kavaz

*Note for actor: Text in **Bold** is spoken to the other person, and regular text is spoken to audience.*

Yasemin I step into the open-plan office like a confident ostrich. It's ten to five and apparently IPA Friday so HR is scavenging for a bottle opener.
It's in his hand. I should say something but –

...an eerily handsome scotch egg is offered to me.

It's vegan?

I shouldn't.

Okay, maybe just one –

Hi!

Five gangly fingers stretch out towards me.

Yes, it's actually Yaz-e-min – I think but don't say, in case that's rude.
She gestures for me to take a seat and as my ass meets the beanbag, I realise, I don't belong here.

How was my day?

It's a tactical way to dissect my interests.

I spent my morning at a Yayoi Kusama exhibition at the Tate.

I've never been to the Tate.
She is, of course, 'a patron' and 'adores the cultural

35

sector'.

I glance at her loafers and notice a birthmark that looks exactly like the figure in *The Scream* painting.

'Well,' she says and straightens her posture. I do nothing to mine.

'So tell me about yourself Yasmin. What could you bring to this role?'

Erm, I –

...don't even own a laptop. Shortcuts? I've got RSI thinking about stretching my hand across the keyboard to reach Shift Command F. Fuck, I mean what am I, beyond the last eight months spent steaming milk at an unrespectable coffee chain.

I'm an optimist.

'Excellent.' Excellent.

She asks me why I am the right fit, and I, I can't stop staring at the expressionist art on her foot. Uncanny.

She notices.

Sorry, I –

...feel myself sinking further into the polystyrene-filled chair.

What was the question?

I think of which Indeed.com's list of desirable qualities I can claim: Self-motivated, meticulous, practical, personable, flexible.

Honest.

She asks me to elaborate and I... sink.

I steal condiments from McDonalds, I burn every cake I make, I eat too much meat, and no I can't hold a downward dog, and yes I pretend I can't hear homeless people, but when I *do* buy them a Tesco meal deal I thrive off the good will for at least a week. And I once killed a bee with a reusable straw. So. Fuck me if I ever crochet a Secret Santa present or naturally use the word 'alas'.

But maybe I'll practise mindfulness and shop sustainably for a pair of those black tapered trousers, go home, iron it and hang it up like a proper adult. Because I'll actually, you know, care about something for once.

Mostly, I could see myself here because I like scotch eggs. Alas, I wish they weren't vegan.

She laughs, and agrees. Thank fuck.

Careers Day
by Eloise Kay

Sam   Is this it? Is this what I've just spent thirty mind-numbing minutes sat at a computer for? Answering stupid questions about whether I prefer numbers or words, and whether I consider myself a 'people person' or not? This is the 'inspiring' and 'thought-provoking' list of possible careers the algorithm has spat out, is it?

Yes, I'm angry, Mr Wilkins. Of *course* I'm angry. Why? Well, let's have a read, shall we? Let's have a gander at the incredible offerings that Craphome Comprehensive's budget career advisor has provided, so we can see exactly how high I'm supposed to aim.

Cleaner.
Bus driver. Prison guard. Mortician.

Mortician! Apparently I'm so shit with people they're suggesting I only deal with them when they're dead! I mean, Jesus Christ, this is meant to put a fire in my belly, is it? Encourage me to scale new heights of academic achievement?

A snob? Are you kidding me? These are the jobs my parents did. My grandparents did. My aunts and uncles and, you know what? Soon my cousins and mates as well, at this rate. If you don't pull your finger out and actually give us some guidance. Or do you secretly believe that we're all just meant to plod along at minimum wage forever? Knowing our place. Having 'realistic' dreams of keeping our heads down and our sights lowered.

Do you think the kids down the road get this, Mr Wilkins? At the posh school with their eye-watering fees and their school trips abroad and their visits from politicians. Do you think the kids there get *these* job suggestions? I don't.

I work bloody hard. Every module, every essay, every extracurricular opportunity. I seize this every single day. No sickies. No lateness. So why can't I get their list of careers, ey?

Is it my surname? Is it my postcode? Or is it you? Is it your Ofsted results that make that computer treat me like a sad statistic?

What are you typing into that computer about me? Do you even know who I am, or what I'm capable of?

Journalist.
Writer.
Teacher.

Nurse.

Pilot. Architect. Psychologist. Politician.

Something that means I get further than the bottom of my street. So I can get out. Don't give me this pile of crap I could have googled in five minutes on Jobs.Gov or whatever and expect me to be grateful.

I've got fire, Mr Wilkins. I need you to give me fuel. I deserve fuel. I demand fuel. And I'm not leaving here till I get it.

Caviar
by Sam Butters

Matty Hold on Katie, love, fuck your mate just say? 'Adorable'? I'm 'adorable'? They think I can't afford to pay, don't they? That's jokes.

You gonna let 'em talk about me – think about me – like that? Course you fuckin' are, I'm just the funny-talkin', Labour leftie bad boy you're dating so that one day you and your posh chums can all look back and laugh about the time you played around in the dirt, which will inevitably make you all feel better about everything being handed to ya. Well, you can all piss off! G'warn! Everyone knows you can't afford this place: either you're just relying on daddy's credit card or the bloke next to you who's chatting you up. Yeah pal, sorry to break it to ya, bottle-blonde Anastasia is only talking to you for the 2-4-1s!

Oh, I'm sorry precious, is this – am I embarrassing you? Yeah? Good! Don't panic, you're safe, I don't think your friends can look down on me any more than they already do. I'll fuck off shall I? Yeah, think I will – and you can take these back. Nah, nah, don't even try, I won't be needing them anymore, poncy fucking keychain anyway. And you can take your, your, caviar – shove that up your pretentious, pristine princessy arse too. Who even likes caviar? Stupid fucking fish brain.

Who were we kidding ay? This wasn't ever gonna work. Let's face facts, Mayfair: I ain't Park Lane or Pret A Manger. I'm Birmingham. I'm state school discos and fizzy pop. I'm football till it's dark and raves until it's light. I'm the rag 'n' bone man and the number 94 man. Man.

I've tried to be a chameleon. A class accommodator camouflaging into my surroundings to this middle-class fuckery, because if you don't, if you don't, you get eaten alive by the predators in the fake, compassionately capitalist rainforest of the ruling class, but fuck all that. Fuck all this and fuck them, and fuck you for preying on me and making me fall in love with you.

I'm shit at lying and I'm shit at being shit and I'm done with feeling out my depth with you. So fucking shallow.

I love you.

It ain't just the shagging, the hanging out with, not just being seen with you – which, I ain't gonna lie to you, it totally was when we first got together – but actually in deep feeling with you.
But people like you, and these, and this whole restaurant, this establishment, this system terrorise me. Look around you, Kate. You think anyone else here is like me? You knew that.

Don't you forget I was enough for you. The air we breathed together, into each other was enough for you. Enough. Until they reappeared out of the jungle and sucked you back in. I love you. So much. Please don't become one of them again. You're better than that. Stronger than that. I've seen it. We're stronger than that.

Checking Out Lucy
by Sam Harry MacGregor

Harry   Oh hi!

(Oh Shit!)

Lucy!

(Lucy, Lucy, Lucy, Lucy...)

Yeah, I've been keeping well, I'm really good thanks.

(For a fucking broken man.)

It's been what, nearly a year?

(335 days and 13 hours since I last heard you say my name.)

I never knew you worked here, must be fairly new then?

(And I have NOT been obsessively daring myself to use your checkout for over a week now. I could not have easily used the self-checkout service today like every other time.)

Yeah, just popped in, needed a few essentials that's all.

(Essentials! Dental floss, self-raising flour, tin of beans and a bag of ice? Not random at all.)

I almost actually didn't recognise you in your uniform!

(Oh my God I want to kiss you.)

You look good though.

(I want to kiss you right here.)

I hope you don't mind…

(Right here in front of everyone. In front of the manager and security. In front of the frozen foods section. Fruit and veg section. Cereals. Shampoos. Everywhere, kiss you everywhere.)

I hope you don't mind me saying that.

(Fuck sake control yourself, boy! This is officially pathetic! Am I sweating? God I'm…)

Yeah, yeah, nah I'm cool, just a bit low on the air conditioning in here, aint it? Err… yes I do need a bag actually, thanks. Bag for life!

(Shut up Harry!)

Yep! I'll use the old contactless please. Thanks.

(I'm sorry I said I hated public displays of affection.)

Has that went through?

(I'm sorry I never held your hand in front of my friends.)

Phew!

(I'm sorry I wasted all our time together when you were all I ever wanted or needed.)

You know when you're just waiting for the payment to go through and you're a bit like aahh…

(STOP talking about contactless fucking payments!)

No, I don't have a Nectar card actually.

(Fuck, I wish I had a Nectar card…I wish it didn't swipe properly and we could be stuck here forever sorting it out. Another customer's coming up behind me. Fuck off! Say something, Harry!)

So yeah… Actually, as soon as we hung up the last time we talked, it hit me like a punch in the face how much I would miss you and it's actually been even worse than that. And I still miss you. I'll never stop missing you. I've never spoke about it to anyone, not really, because the only one I've ever been able to talk to was you. IS you. And I know you're at work and this is really inappropriate, but the truth is I'm not alright. I don't want the receipt and I don't want none of this shit I'm buying or a bag for life. I just want you…for life.

(Say something Harry. Say anything… Speak!).

Checkout
by Ellen Lilley

BRITNEY at the checkout starts to scan.

Britney Heinz. *(Beat.)* Heinz! Bloody hell, Martha, you got
the queen coming 'round like? I never thought I'd
see the day. You should have asked if there was any
smart price in the back. I kna Dazza pretends not to
hear people say 'excuse me', but he would have
went if you asked him. I wonder if you'll be able
to tell the difference. *(Laughs.)* You know, in my
primary school they would put snide tomato sauce
into Heinz bottles. AS IF WE WOULDN'T NOTICE. I
said to Julie – me fave dinner lady – 'Howay man,
we're not tramps, I can't enjoy my smiley faces with
this shit.' She agreed.

*Looks up and realises tears are streaming down Martha's
face.*

Martha... oh, Martha. *(Panics.)* Come on now, not
here. My head is still banging from last night, I've
only slept two hour and a quarter. Pack it in. Put
those tears away. Where's this came from?

Thank god you've got your rich teas – you've not
totally lost it. Someone died? Or *(mouths)* is it the
menopause, is it? I know it's awful. My mam broke
down when she realised a bag for life had longer
left than she does!

Beat.

> Shit. It's the beans, I should have known. Martha, I'll refund them and get Dazza –

Looking at Martha.

> What's that on your arms?

> It's him, isn't it?

To someone in the queue:

> Oy! You don't even start. Aisle six is empty.

> Right, Look at me. This needs to stop. You used to waltz in here like Nigella Lawson on a budget. Martha. *(Beat.)* You haven't even got your mascara on. Fuck's sake.

> No Martha, stop it, I'm fine. That wasn't meant to make you worse.

> Like 'em...? I dunno. I did once treat myself to some heels that weren't from Primark – thought I was the dog's bollocks. But you know what? They absolutely killed. *(Beat.)* Before every night out my mam makes me promise two things, right?

> 1) I won't touch stray dogs.

> 2) I'll NEVER walk barefoot in the street.

> I couldn't believe the audacity of these expensive shoes sabotaging my night so I HAD to take them

off. But the worst part is, I felt genuine guilt and shame at the sight of my dirty rotten feet in the morning. 'Cause that's not me, Martha. I don't let myself down like that. I dance with pride the full fucking night long in my cheap heels and Do. Not. Stop. Anyways, next morning I threw all thirty quid's worth of them in the bin. Lesson learned for life.

What I'm saying, Martha, is some things just isn't worth it. We all have standards, but when you start lowering your own for other things or people? That's just sad. Proper sad. It's a disservice to your self-worth. Yeah, we're all allowed a bare foot moment, but how we walk on after is what matters the most.

Beat.

Fucking hell, listen to me! I'm a therapist when I'm hanging, apparently.

To the queue:

I SAID AISLE SIX MAN!

Coming Out
by Paul Culshaw

Adam   Mum, Dad… I've been lying to ya. I'm still Adam, but I'm a different Adam… Cos y'see… the truth of the matter is… The… truth…

I'm Tory.

I'm… a Tory.

I know this is going to come as a huge shock and I've packed a bag, I can go and stay with a friend if you want me to leave. But if you allow me to re-main here, I'm no flag waver! I'm not gonna put a big 'Vote Conservative' sign up in me window. I'd never bring shame or trouble to your door or make us the talk of the estate. Dad, I've overheard you say how you feel about us, as people. 'Dirty Tories'. I've stayed silent through all of the digs and the jibes.

Do you have any idea how it feels? To feel that you love everything about me apart from… a part of who I am? What I do in the privacy of my own ballot booth is my business. I preferred when all of this remained private – I find it uncouth, arguing about it all over Facebook – my point being, this doesn't define who I am. I can't pretend to hate BoJo any-more. I haven't been lying to you, I've just had to… bend the truth a bit. Haven't we all at some point?

I know you don't meet many people like me around here, not in this neck of the woods. I can't go on pretending I was watching *The Iron Lady* solely for Meryl Steep. You sent me to a posh school! God, that came out so wrong. I'm not blaming you. This is about me, it's not you, it's me. I never liked milk at school anyway!

I've been this way for a long time y'know. It's not a phase, like that time I went semi-vegan for a week. And Mum, those Jo Malone scented candles – that wasn't a gay thing, I actually just like luxury. I enjoy horse-riding. It's true, every time Dad suspected I was going to a chemsex party at weird times on a Sunday afternoon, I admit that I was taking the car without permission on journeys I knew I shouldn't. I was skipping through fields of wheat riding Theodore…. me mate's horse.

Do you know how stressful it's been hiding all of me *Daily Mail*s in the back of the closet, burying them in a sea of back issues of *Attitude*, pretending to enjoy *The Guardian*?

Our Ian's known for a while. Threatened to out me. Caught me eating hummus watching *The Great British Bake-Off* – I had to pay him to stop him grassing me up – and Ma, I know you knew something was off when I got excited about the *Strictly* results! And seeing as we're spilling it *all* out on the table, I actually love the Queen!

You'll never know what it's like to walk a mile in my Oxford Brogues. To lie in bed with your headphones on in the fear you'd find out I wasn't watching re-runs of *RuPaul's Drag Race* and all this time I've been secretly binge watching *The Crown*. I know this is a lot to take in – but Dad, I just want to be clear on one thing. The whole 'Tory' thing... it has absolutely nothing to do with my love of tweed. I rock that jacket! I've been given compliments on it on nights out in Hoxton *and* Belgravia. I've been told that I looked sharp! Whatever happens, whatever you decide... if there's just one thing... please remember that I am very much still your son. That hasn't changed. Not to me. I just have a different set of priorities. Things that are important to me. I do care about the economy. I just... prefer to travel first class.

COONCIL (KID)
by Amber Sinclair-Case

JAY – Mid 20s, any ethnicity, male identifying.

Jay   Junkie? Listen mate, I dae ken what you hink a
junkie constitutes, but it's no me. A junkie hangs
aboot on shop corners beggin fur money from people tryin to get thur messages. A junkie invites him-
sel to your party so he can chor all your bucky. A
junkie hinks if he has aner line he doesny have tae
take a shower. I'm no a junkie. A went ti uni. Business management. Did awright. No the best, but
didny get kicked oot so. I ken ma accent makes me
sound like a junkie but that's Leven fur ye. A junkie
ca think straight. Piss poor. Too worried aboot the
next fix. That's no me. Am still in ma student grants.
Big greens, mate. They always called me the cooncil
kid at uni. No far off te be fair.

Ma first day, I walked inty register wi ma student
number nd that, feelin fly as fuck. I walked in wearin
my best trainers, Jordans that I'd saved up for fir
yonks, white as anyhin. Baseball cap oan, boiler suit
zipped up. A ken what that soonds like but I thought
I'd have tae prove masel. Prove that am hard, like.
Anyway. I didny. I walked into a bunch eh posh
twats in their balenciarmas wi fuckin diamond en-
crusted phone cases an that. Clutchin their steam
pressed registration papers like they were copies of

the American amendments. Wi me on the er side pullin them oot my trackie pocket. Tangled in ma headphones. Empty fag packet faws oot on the floor tae. Boggin. Eyes on me. Minded me eh the skel. The way the teacher used tae look at me like a was some sorta diseased rat. I looked wan eh the balenciarmas in the face, right. Gearin mysel up to say somethin proper wideo, eh. 'Where'd ye get they from?' 'Selfridges. Limited Edition.' 'Aw aye, av been there, that's where a recognise them.' Balenciarma looked. We both knew I didny. No like I didny wanty go and blow my pocket money on chunky creps. No like I didny want tae run ti mummy and daddy whenever I needed an extra fifty quid. Like ma maw could afford fags fur me, let alone trainers. Feelin fly as fuck in that hall wi ma Jordans then Ciarma from Morninside made me feel like av always felt. Aw still hink I'm a pig shit, piss poor rat.

I ken. Get er yersel. Wan hing we could agree on wis the Scots tradition of getting as steamin as possible. Some eh the English lads had never tried bucky. Or MD. Their idea of a shot was a soorz. Tragic, mate. But aye, uni was awright. I did it. Got ma degree. More than a junkie would, anaw.

Anyway, what's a couplea gram eh sniff tae you anyway. I dinny take it hardcore like. Just when I need it. Been goin through it recently man, so aye. Am takin my bit more than usual. Whit does it have tae do wi you?

Actually mate, can you make it two g? Just cause a might have my job in a couple days and that, so a canny come back and get more. Honest. A ken a said that yesterday but a dropped it doon the toilet mind. Here, kin you do me a favour? Dae tell any-one am here man. Ave got a reputation. I'm no fucking junkie.

Date Night
by Jordan John

Craig   She places her hand on top of the bill.
Not *her* hand, not really. It used to belong to her.
Now it floats through the air as if held by a piece of
string. Like it might crumble.

The sun shines through the window, skimming
through chandeliers, and this single ray of light
kisses her hand as if it were meant for her.
It's this cream that she uses. Makes her hands
glisten. Expensive but worth it she says. Keeps her
skin from wrinkling. I keep my hands in my pockets.
Fuck! Waiter's coming over.
I swiftly place my hand on the bill.
Jagged, coarse. On top of hers. She doesn't react to
the sweat, but in her eyes this touch means some-
thing else.
No honestly babe, I got this.
The waiter's by her side now.
Says he'll give us a minute.

She got promoted see.
I squeezed myself into this suit for this occasion, for
her, for this place – Do you like it? I ask.
The dress to impress, I mean.
The mask I mean.
Do you like how it hugs me?
Fits me rather snugly, albeit slightly tightly around

the neckline.
I don't want you to think I'm defined by the bread-
line
So, when I say that I got this, I mean I got this.
Let me get this.
Baby. This. Your day. Let me get this.
A chorus of eyes. Watching. Judging. We see you
and we don't buy it. This is a zoo and you are an
animal in a cage. Poking, prodding, glasses clanging
together in synchrony like it's rehearsed. A perfor-
mance. Every laugh, practiced. Every flourish of the
wrist planned. The air here is bought and paid for
and you sir do not belong.
I shuffle.
Politely.

The charlatan oozing out of the expensive seams,
it's scary really, how this costume contains me.
She sees the cufflinks; a different kind of bling and
she's pleased that my shoes shine but ashamed
how the tag pokes out of the collar.
Did you rent that suit? she asks.
The waiter makes a timely appearance again.
Did you rent that suit? A little too loudly this time.
The restaurant quietens.

It's not just pride that keeps my hand on hers,
Some hopeless idea that the woman I once recog-
nised might come back to me.

I feel frowned on.

Abstract.

Like I don't exist.

For the first time I really look at her.

From her heels to the tip of her nose.

Is that rented? I ask.

Is that a borrowed look?

She draws the bill closer

Her eyes start to water. Please don't make a scene.

She's just climbing the ranks.

I'm inclined to disagree as I realise that this is the
last time we will be.

I tell her I love her.

But the path she's taking strays from who she really
is.

I tell her that I've never really been one for pretending

And that keeping up appearances sounds exhaust-
ing

And as the ray of sunshine moves on to the next
table and the light around her dims a little, I notice

How tired she looks.

Her hand on the bill

My hand on hers

Please, she begs

Let me have this.

Description
by Winnie Imara

Lade 'That girl LOVES plantain! She can eat plantain for days! Plantain waffle, plantain pancake, plantain burger, plantain chips, plantain lasagne, plantain every-tinnnnn!'
'Disney lover, knows absolutely every word to *Finding Dory*, every word!'
'Caring.'
'Great Listener.'
'Lights up the room...'
That is how my friends and family describe me.

When I asked management why I was being dismissed, you know what they said? 'You fit the description.' That the CCTV showed someone entering our manager's office and I fit that description.

I asked to see the camera footage. But they ignored me and continued reading out this statement they made against me.

I knew something was up for months, when they kept checking everything I did, no explanation, just 'procedure'.

So when they called me into that meeting room, and I saw them all sitting there, managers, security... my heart started beating and I just knew – I knew it had nothing to do with some blurry grainy video footage, just my skin.

My skin always fits the description.

They started bringing up all these other allegations, saying that I was aggressive at work, that I was un-professional, that I didn't 'fit in with the team', and when I tried to object, they said I was argumenta-tive, I always looked angry, had attitude, was rude to clients, and the more I tried to defend myself they more they said that I was shouting, which I wasn't – 'Angry' 'aggressive' 'unprofessional' over and over.

And I had tried so hard. To smile. All the time. To let the 'comments' slide... but... I had to think about why I was there, where I wanted to get to, and not letting anything stop that.

I am here because... I want change, I want everyone who looks like me, talks like me, to be safe and se-cure when they're at work, because every single one of them deserves to be respected for their edu-cation, experience, hard work and basic humanity... they deserve to be safe. We all have the right to feel safe. Wherever we are.

I know this will be hard. I know this will be long. And I know there is a chance we might lose. But at least we can fight. And if you're able to help, I think we can help change the conversation. At least we'll have done something towards making things better. It's not about the money. I'm just sick of sitting at home feeling helpless.

I'm ready to fight. That's the description I want.

Devil
by Vanessa Schofield

LOLA sits in a prison visitor's room. She is nervous but determined. Sat opposite her is a young man who is a prison inmate.

Lola   You... still... somehow creep into my dreams every night. I've tried all sorts to stop it. Chamomile tea, white wine, red wine, readin' before bed, wankin' before bed. Nothin' has worked. Especially not the wankin': you slip in somehow, join me in my slumber.

There's this thing that keeps happenin' and I need – I need it to stop. It's called erm, sleep paralysis? It's where you wake up but can't move. They say it's like havin' an evil spirit in the room.

The devil sat on your chest.

You can't breathe.

You can't move.

Your whole body is frozen.

And your mind, your mind is sayin': Move. Scream. Run.

But you can't. So you just lie there, frozen with fear. And take it. Prayin' that it will be over soon. History repeats itself. Even in dreams. Endless timeless horror. I googled it. 'Not being able to move when awake but also asleep.' Somehow. Loads of people experience it, apparently. Trauma can bring it on... There's this paintin' of it from like, the olden days.

Sleep paralysis. It's trippy as fuck. There's this horse watchin' as the devil squats on this woman's naked body. And she looks so helpless.

You're in here, locked up, behind bars. Trapped. Livin' your own little nightmare. And yet somehow you manage to invade me again and again and again...

Sometimes someone will look at me on the bus, for a second too long. And I panic – have they seen the video? Have they seen my face before? At job interviews. What if this person has got kicks from me – pleading No. No. No. Look at me.

LOOK AT ME.

I'm not like the woman in the paintin'. A damsel in distress, captured in oils. You see I am in control now. Keys between knuckles make me feel powerful on a walk home, not terrified. I refuse to be... I don't need to know why you... why you chose me... why you...

Do you believe in God?

I do. An eye for an eye.

What you did to me...

I hope there are people doin' that to you. In here. Every. Single. Day.

I came here today... to forgive you. To look you in the eye and let the pain go.

But how do I forgive the devil?

Dickhead
by Jane Ryan

Ali   I can't say that. They'll think I'm a right dickhead.

God, why am I here? I thought I would be painting not sitting around and… and… talking.

I didn't think a night class would be so much… pressure.

And can someone tell me who the fuck named this 'Feeling Week' and decided it was a good idea to go around the class one by one and… communicate… formulate, and what else did they call it? Enunciate. Talking wank about our *relationship* to the piece.

Everyone just… sitting, trying to look like they're really looking at *Blue Monochrome* by Yves Klein.

I'm two people away from having to speak. My knee can't sit still.

Camilla is so… elegant. She's really enjoying herself. Do I look like I'm enjoying myself? Smile. Go on, Smile. Too much. They'll get suspicious. Smaller. Lift the corners a bit. Maybe lean an elbow. Rest your head? Like everyone else hanging onto her every word…

It's speaking to me, really speaking, yah, yah… it's actually screaming out… She pauses… *about the immaterial values in which…* Wait for it, she's still going… *we are unable to physically feel, yah.*

(Clapping.) Aren't we all, Camilla? Aren't. We. All?

Total confidence. Good on her.

But I can't speak. I don't want to speak. Especially in front of all these… coz when I speak, yeah… it sounds like… it doesn't sound like them.

Oh fuck. One more person left before me.

Be intellectual. What did Goethe say? Something like, 'when rooms are full of blue, they feel bigger but also cold and empty.'

How strange that blue should make me feel so warm. So protected. The colour reminds me of when those Renaissance artists painted Madonna and Child. Does that make sense? All dressed and coloured in that particular type of blue. You know what I mean? Like… Botticelli. Oh, I love Botticelli. Oh, oh, or like Bellini.

And now… I'm getting a feeling and I don't know how to describe it. It says so much and nothing at all.

Like, I'm not contemplating the authenticity of truth like the rest of them. Nothing highly intellectual about me. I just love what I love when I see it!

I can't say that. They'll think I'm a right dickhead.

Why do people have to talk about art, though? Shouldn't we just do it and appreciate it... ourselves, like? The artists themselves create with their hands. Like a cleaner... an electrician... but unlike the cleaner, artists can paint strokes in whatever direction they want.

Now what am I on about?

Shit... I'm next... wait. It's me.

They're all looking at me.

My face is so red. It mixes with the blue. The whole room grows purple.

Take your time... I can do this... Show them you... you belong here.

My mouth opens.

I answer: I don't know. Nothing. I've got nothing.

Dickhead.

Dog Mum

by Nieve Hearity

Millie   God you're putting me on the spot. Er, okay, I've got this slightly weird medical condition.

It's called tokophobia.

It's the pathological fear of pregnancy and child-birth.

And... I've got it.

Oh, I adore children, I would love to have them – I just don't want to be pregnant or give birth to them.

I don't think it has anything to do with the 'right' guy even though you are lovely! Just the thought of being pregnant ooh I've come over all queasy.

Pauses, swallowing back a gag.

I was never a kid person, but I think it was in school when it properly started. They showed us a birth video in biology, that bloody Mister Stephens – he'd do anything to get out of actually teaching a class.

Look, I thought we'd just see the woman's face as she pushed, but they parked a camera between her legs, yelled action and let it roll.

The screams still haunt me.

The agony on her face as she pushed a bowling ball out of her distorted vagina.

My vagina is reserved for tampons and bad decisions.

So, this lump rips out of her, covered in blood and mucus – Oh God I've gone funny again, give me a minute. *(Exhales heavily.)* Jesus.

Sorry, where was I? Oh yeah, then the doctor hands It to her and she's smiling at this shrieking crotch demon, legs akimbo as they stitch up her Frankenpussy, like this is normal?

The whole thing is a shitshow, it's just so unnatural. Only a man could have come up with it – probably those Romans, I've seen *Caligula*!

Sorry?

Well, yes, I am a mum, just not of a baby, I mean he's my baby – my beagle: Baxter. I get to be a mummy without the trauma.

Yes, I know it's not the same, it's better!

Baxter is always happy to see me; even on my worst days he cheers me up. We never argue. I don't have to yell at him to tidy up, he listens. And he loves me so much; do you know how wonderful that is? All the benefits of being a mum, of loving him and watching him grow but without all the horror of actually having a baby.

And the best part? When Baxter dies, I can just get another dog.

Estate of Mind
by Karen Whyte

TONI – any gender; age 25+.

Toni   I love how much you love Oprah.
When Oprah's on, 11 a.m. till 12 noon, we all knew
it was protected time and that no one was allowed
to speak. You had a proper little ritual about it.
Washing up has to be done, laundry hung up (probably on the edge of dodgy from last night's wash),
and your tea freshly brewed. Earl Grey, cos you like
to get a bit fancy when it's Queen O on the telly. I
remember sometimes you getting your notepad out
to scribble sayings and that that Oprah would come
out with.

In the summer holidays you'd send me off with my
little brothers to play, armed with water guns and
enough for a 99 each, and we'd head off downstairs
into the concrete jungle feeling as rich as you could
be. God, those summers! Ice cream starting to run
down your hand before it had even met your face
kind of heat. Hosing down the concrete floor in the
block so it wouldn't burn your feet when the floor
really was lava. Smokey BBQs filling the air and that
first delicious moment of absolute bliss as the sun
meets your skin and everything and anything feels
possible.

Most of the time you'd be fine on the Ferrier. It was more the posh boys from the grammar school down the road that got their stuff stolen. Well, I don't even know if you could call it 'stolen', really. Big Mike would just ask for it, and whoever would just hand it over. Bags, trainers, phones – no questions asked. Big Mike was such a gentle giant. He'd never been in a fight himself, but you knew that if he ever did he could fucking floor anyone without even try-ing. The guy was stacked, wasn't he! 6 foot 4 at six-teen years old and he could lift just about anything.

He stayed with us for a few months. His mum wasn't too well; she was always about 12 steps away from him, if you get me. I remember saying he could borrow mine if he liked.
Everyone knew you as Mummy Christine.

I remember one time Big Mike left a fist-shaped hole in the kitchen wall after his mum cancelled on a visit. She left him waiting, with his cleaned nails and in his freshly ironed shirt, perched upright like he was in church, for two hours before her sponsor rang the flat to say she wasn't coming.

For a few seconds after, he was motionless. Then he started pacing, legs not knowing where they were going but picking a direction, any direction, full steam ahead. Then he cried out a noise I'd never heard before, like a wounded animal. I couldn't place whether he was more frustrated with her or with himself for hoping. One hand finding the kitchen wall for stability, trying to collect his thoughts, and the other tore off his shirt from the collar, buttons running for cover, his hand clenched up in a fist and boom. Debris fell at his feet and he crumbled, crying. These huge beads of hot salty tears rolling down his cheeks. He was so ashamed when he broke the news to you. And you, my tiny mum, just opened your arms and cradled all 6 foot 4 of him. You rocked him and told him not to worry about the wall. You actually said how thoughtful he was by giving the plasterer a job to do! We all laughed. Snot, tears and smiles all rolled into one. That was you all over. I mean warmth radiated out of every pore. That's why everyone gravitated towards you. We couldn't help it. We were like moths to a flame and you, you were the light in all this. In everything.

One thing you said to Big Mike that night has really stuck with me, and I actually found it written down in one of your notebooks last week. You said we have to 'turn our wounds into wisdom', that it doesn't happen overnight, but day by day you get there.

So that's what I've been trying to do since you passed, and I'm still waiting for any wisdom to show up.

I've started watching re-runs of Oprah though, just to feel a bit closer to you.

And yeah. It's helping.

Eyes Up
by Gail Egbeson

Theo   Look here, yeah, up in my eyes. I am sick and tired of your games. See, I've tried to be civil – but since you wanna play, let's play!

Don't sit there acting like you don't know what I mean. Talking 'bout, what's my name? you see me here every month like clockwork. The only difference today is there's no Maccie D's bag 'cause, surprise surprise, I don't even have 99p to buy a bloody hash brown.

I'm here each last Friday of the month, and even though you claim to open at 9 a.m. I don't complain when I find myself patiently waiting out in savage weather when you finally unlock the doors at 9.15. Trying to ignore all the vaguely curious stares from passers-by, judging me as if they know every decision that made me end up at your mercy.

I come here every month, queue like a good citizen, get to your counter, state my name, how much I want, lie about my expenses, and all the while your eyes never leave that keyboard. I stand and wait patiently for you to type whatever it is that you pretend to type and eventually hand over the 390 you could easily round up to 400 – but hey, I don't complain.

What does this have to do with my application? Oh, you're all spicy now, innit. Getting excited at seeing a black man at the edge of surrender? Savouring the spectacle of how money can humble a man? Well, one day, my friend, you'll look and actually see me at this counter and wish you'd paid more attention all these years as I humble you.

I'm sorry, I know you're just doing your job. Already a long day and it's not even started. Feelin your pain. Working at nightshift ain't easy uno. Specially on the confectionary aisle. Steve says I'm well behind on sales targets but I don't let that kill my vibe and neither will you as long as you run me the cheque. I need these extra pennies, man.

Shit, I'm rambling, kinda nervous, there's bare people here, it's usually just you and me. Okay cool, let's start with my name. Why don't we just call me 'Super', surname 'Star', and put that in flashing lights? What, you don't get it? What's wrong with you? A bit of banter, not flirting with you.

Ah! I get it, I see what this is. It tickles your ego knowing I can't go nowhere else. I mean a 73 credit score shuts all doors, but that ain't got nothing on the Lidl for Loans spiral I'm caught in, so here's what we're not gonna do. You're gonna stop blanking me like you don't know who I am and start showing some respect, and I ain't gonna hold it over you that I pay your wages. That's right, where do you think the 32.7% interest I pay on my loans goes to? Yeah, you!

You know what, bun this. You're wasting my time. I'll get through this without you. Mark this moment, I'm ending this cycle. I promise you'll miss this face. I'm going. See me going?

Aren't you gonna say something? What was that?

Listen, If you're gonna say it, then look me in the face. Look at me! I said LOOK AT ME! EYES UP!!

Flying Too Close to The Son
by Sam Purkis

MARKY's dad was a gangster. Marky's dad is now dead. Marky has something to say, so he locks his brother in the shed for the funeral.

Marky   Flowers are for people that enjoy life, James. You should've brought him something sickly and poisonous. Or just cyanide. When something rots, you cut it away so the living parts aren't tainted. You've always been the gentle one, but you think that's your achievement, no mate, that's mine. Do you know what it's like to hold something so tight in your chest that it affects – nah – *inf*ects your mind and body? I can feel my body tighten all day. Do you know what it's like to have your mum tell your family she's scared of you or whisper it on the phone to her wine-stinkin' friends? I was always so gentle around her. She's like crockery, so fragile, and either so valuable and perfectly put together that only an expert should handle it, or just a knock off that may end up cutting a child. Little parasites.

I was the only fucker in the family that would stand up to him, the bully that heads the house, the one that all the other little household bullies across the country cower over. Do you know what I had to do to myself to do that? I stripped everything I loved about myself away. I stripped myself of my own

77

voice and adopted his – did away with childish laughter and learned how to brood and snarl to stop our father pushing you into fucking cutting yourself again. I figured out young that he's only ever been frightened of himself, and I morphed into him for you. Who would you sacrifice your tenderness for? You're so fucking ungrateful and Mum, she can't fucking stand me. She watched me break myself for this cause and now she has the fucking gall to hate me. Overreacting to everything I do or say like it weren't inevitable.

Remember how much I used to chatter? Grandad would pay me to shut up. I'd do *Planet Earth* narrations on bugs – I'm not done. You're gonna hear everything I did for you. I learnt how to throw a mean fucking punch so I could pull him off you or Mum or T. I can't go there today and listen to people talk about him all affectionate like he wasn't a cunt.

The saddest thing about his death is that he went too quickly. I'd barely started. I wanted a cut for each time he was a cunt. He was always a cunt. I was gonna sculpt gills to match his slime. The bitch choked it after eight, should've expected that. The time I needed his violent stubbornness he pissed off into serenity. I kept looking at him, waiting for him to fight. He was so pathetically human. I tried to leave but I'd already started cutting. He looked like grade A fillet steak when I finished. Dad just needed to be dead to be beautiful.

I became violent so you could run your pacifist routine, guess what else I learned? That nobody punches like him. Except me. You've got to get in the ring at Madison Square Garden on a Saturday night to feel that kind of force.

I trained up. I'd walk around the worst places. Remember where that kid got gutted on New Road? I spent the next week walking down there tryna find trouble. That girl getting raped down the alley near One Stop? Patrolled there too. I knew no one contender could match Dad – ogre – so I needed to test myself against every single gutter monster to slay the dragon, a 5 foot 9, beer-stained red-faced dragon. What a shit fairytale. None of you ever helped me on that crusade and I never asked you to, cos I knew it had to be just me. You weren't built for it, just cried every time, six years older than me for fuck sake, a whole 23 years old, running from the tea-table leaving soggy fucking potato smilies and fish fingers.

I could have hated you, could have thought fucking pathetic useless worm and left you to be destroyed. But I never did. I loved you. And Mum. I'm not asking for your love in return, I gave up on that years back. What I want is for you to acknowledge what I've done for you, and for once in your life say thank you. And you are not leaving that fucking shed until you do.

Free School Meal
by Dominic Holmes

Dominic   I were a child genius you know.
Not your run of the mill quiz show
lad – like actual, IQ through the roof,
mind-bending , dog's bollocks,
attending Oxbridge at 11
type of shit
Which, I understand it
sounds like I'm bullshitting on this one
And I might be, but – look at my face
No go on, look,
Look

Me mam says I've got trusting eyes
Moss green, which is soothing
But it's mainly the lazy eye drooping
lower with each
tick
of the clock
makes people stop
and laugh at the brain box.
Little bastard though
Skinny frame, cheeky smile
Hand me down uniform, second-hand style
with ears like Dumbo, FA cup – picked up
and paraded to the rest of the school
'Look at his shoes though'

I could've been anything Doctor, Astronaut
but I thought
All I ever want to be
is a Dinner Lady.
Hairnet, pinnie, apron
That's the life for me.
Best people in school they were.
Keeper of the keys.
Feeders, leaders, providers of nutrition
Always smiling
Always giving
Especially Mrs Gregson.
She were the head Dinner Lady

 Massive smile. Gold tooth,
which meant she was a witch obviously
but I didn't care,
she were my best mate and I were
lacking
in that department.
She had a thing for the free school mealers,
gave us extra portions, she knew how to feed us.
'Eat up lad, you've a long walk home.
Get some fire in that belly
Get some meat on those bones'
She'd drive past me in the mornings
On the way to her shifts
I thought if she's really that bothered

She'd give me a lift.
You know
But,
I'd do it for her
I'd work up that appetite
Agree on the deal
Because there's really no such thing as a free school
meal.

Gateway to the Soul

by Connor Allen

Ashley   C'mon then, I'll take on both of you!

My mum always said that the eyes are the gateway
to the soul.
You can tell a lot about a person by the look in their
eyes, she'd say. What they're thinking
How they're feeling
Their intentions
Their desires
It's all there, in their eyes.
Both of your eyes are telling me that even though
there's two of you, and you got an advantage with
that blade in this skinny prick's hand
you're out of your depth
Got no place being here
In this alleyway
With me and my bike.
Trying to take the one thing that is irreplaceable
from a madman with nothing to lose.

Yeah, there's doubt in those eyes
And that's the worst thing to have
Doubt
Questioning what move to make
And whether you have what it takes to do what's
necessary. Because I can promise you right now
It ain't going to go down how you hope.

You ain't got it in you
To be that certain type of person who'll do what's
necessary and hold no remorse for rash actions
No care
No guilt

No doubt
That you can wake up every morning and look in the
mirror and be OK with who's looking back.

You rolled up on the wrong guy today. You really
did.

Too many wannabes these days. Roaming the
streets
Thinking they're bad boys. Gangsters.

Trying to jack a man's bike
My bike!
The only thing I got left of my mamma
The last thing she left me
And you think you just gunna run up on man and
take that from me?

You'll have to do what's necessary

Because there's no doubt in these eyes. I've known
for time that I'm different
That I've got what it takes to survive.
To *do* what it takes to survive

That I don't give a shit about the consequences
And who gets in my way.

I've done unforgivable things to those closest to me.
To those who loved me and raised me

Now, If I can do that to them and be OK when I look
in the mirror, what d'you think I'll do to you pair of
pussies? HUH!?
Look into my eyes and tell me I'm lying
Tell me I'm bluffing.
Because this is going to go one of two ways...

Either one, you give me my bike, put the knife away
and get the fuck outta my sight or two, I'll take that
knife outta your hand and take my bike anyway
along with both your lives. Your choice.

And seeing as it's my birthday I'll be generous and
give you to the count of three

One... Two...

Three.

Gluten Free
by Adil Hassan

Mo Mum, it ain't my fault I can't eat anything here!
The GP told me try cutting out gluten, so that's
what I'm doing. Why? So I can stop shitting so
much! I'm late to everything because I keep having
to take a shit all the time. Long, endless painful
shits, with you complaining that I take too long in
the toilet. And now I'm trying to fix up, you still ain't
happy.

It's not funny, Mum. I've had enough. Let alone the
physical pain. Can't get to college on time, can't get
to work on time, and when I finally manage to make
it there I need to go every hour or so. Oh, and the
never-ending, proper stinky farts that choke you.
It's toxic, cancerous – you know how bad it gets. It's
ruining the reputation I've never even had. I'm
known for being the late guy and the... gotta poo
guy. People think I'm being selfish, careless, show-
ing off. I don't wanna make an entrance, I don't
want attention, I literally don't want to give... a shit.
I just want to have a normal life doing normal stuff
without random, sudden bowel movements stopping me in my tracks.

I've tried no dairy – didn't work; tried fasting, juic-
ing, low fibre, no fibre, and now I'm trying no gluten
and I would appreciate some consideration!

I know I sound like those boujee posh people who shop at Wholefoods... but I'm just a poor desperate bastard who wants to know what's it's like to have just a casual, scentless fart a day, or a little shit before I go to bed. Nothing excessive. Is that too much to ask?

I'm not shouting! You're shouting! Why you shouting? Why are you angry at me? I ain't being picky. What do you not understand? I literally cannot eat this! I know it's a special occasion. I can see that there's people here. You care too much what people think. I told you specially in advance, I can't eat anything with gluten, and it's like you deliberately put in an extra effort to cook everything you could think of containing gluten to punish me.

No, it ain't that simple, bruv. No, you shut up! And you can sit down an' all, nobody's talking to you. No, not you Mama. Everyone shut up! Oh my days, literally nobody understands.

Okay, Fine! Look Mama, I'm eating it, look mmmm, gluten... Now expect me to shit in my bed.

No I'm not gonna apologise. Why do we even have all these guests? Who are all these people? I don't even know half of them and it's supposed be my bloody birthday. Everyone knows your stinky son Mo ain't got any friends anyway.

Don't you start! I ate some didn't I? Oh my – listen, Aunty, I don't know if you're my aunty aunty but you can fuck off home now, alright? Party over. Yeah, I know, I'm out of order! I'm always out of order. I'm always irritable, I've got irritable bowels! And oops, here we go, I've just shat myself again – gosh, so sorry, don't blame me – blame the bloody gluten!

Growing Out
by Rachelle Grubb

Jess   'Calm down'? Did you just actually tell me to calm down? What? You don't want your new mates to know that your best mate of ten fuckin' years has travelled all the way from the other side of London to come and celebrate your fuckin' birthday. Do you see how this lot were staring at me when I came in? Looking at me like I was gunna rob the fuckin' place. Like I'm not good enough to be 'ere.

You're supposed to be my mate, 'ave my back... and now you're tellin' me that I've got to 'calm down'? Fuck you. Fuck them and Fuck you...

At least I turned up. The others all said bollocks to that. They warned me not to come, begged me not to make a mug of meself, with you acting like you actually wanted us 'ere.

Do these lot 'ere even know you? Cos the reeeeaal you didn't go to some fancy boarding school or on poncey skiing trips to Austria or Switzerland or whatever. The real you didn't 'ave no holiday home in the south of fuckin' France and the real you wouldn't be havin' some sad party at a shit-don't-stink club in Chelsea. Sippin' on champagne, pre-tendin' that you belong 'ere, when two years ago we was drinkin' Strongbow out the bottle on the kids' swings and livin' off other people's fag ends. Sayin' that we weren't never gunna be like them.

You don't 'ave to be like them, man, not for me.

Come home, man. Where you ain't never had to hide who you are. Hanging out in the park where you can just… be. 'Avin' a real laugh…

No amount of success will eclipse the shit we've been through… Renting some wannabe penthouse now like you're the big man. Big bollocks Nick the banker… blanking a past that you wish didn't matter. Well, it does. The clothes you wear 'n' how you do your hair won't change who you are and what you've been and what you've done. You can front all you like but it'll always be 'ere… The fear… the fear of what these people would do if they knew. How they'd see you if they sussed out that you weren't one of them…

Yeah, you're still more like me, ain't you? Stood standin' here lookin' in and wonderin', where's he gone? The kid that could run and run and never get caught. The kid who didn't give a toss what people thought. Close up the grass might still look greener but you ain't freer, mate. Fake your smiles to them lot all you like.

Don't tell me to calm down! Fuck off! *(Waving a*

glass away.) And you can fuck off with that champagne shit! If I don't get a pint of Strongbow in my hand right now, I'll show your posh chums who they're really messin' with and you can calm them down!

Hey thingy! Waiter! Strongbow, please! Now!

Healthy Heart
by Nicole Joseph

A hospital room in West Yorkshire. JAN, 37, grapples with her 20-year-old son, who she is visiting.

Jan   Just like that? Four years and you're just shrugging your shoulders? This girl worships you and you're dumping her like shit in a toilet bowl. Yeah, okay, all this might not be your fault, but you don't have to take it out on her, do ya? Being a single mum wa' a bastard, but I said, smile through it, Jan, he won't always be a little shit. I thought I'd bring you up to be a decent bloke but look at ya. You're just like your father!

Don't you think I wanted to quit and live the life of Riley? I never let you see how hard it wa'. That wa' my mistake, cos you obviously think it's *so* easy that you're gonna leave this girl to do it all on her own. Not on my watch, Sonny Jim!

It's not your fault you're ill, but it's no excuse. This illness is a part of you, has been for years. It's no one else's fault you can't man up and deal with it. How could you not tell your own girlfriend? I thought yer bowels were dodgy, not your heart! You might be in pain, but pregnancy's no picnic either, especially when you've been abandoned. I don't know what goes on inside your head but whatever it is, you can't go around destroying things, people. Breaking this girl's heart, putting yourself in hospital, you're sending my blood pressure through the roof! You're about to bring a fatherless baby boy into the world. You – *my* baby boy.

I couldn't even recognise that little boy now. The boy who could do no wrong in my eyes, so clever for his age. I always wondered where he got it from.

Now, I see. You got nothing from me.

I Saw a Boy Hug His Dad
by Amin Ali

Shahid I saw a boy hug his dad at the train station today...
I forgot that love could exist
Between a man and his father.
I felt so jealous. I could've broke down and burst
out crying. Right there. At Euston, during rush hour.

Why did you stop loving me?
When I was a boy you'd tell me you love me. You'd
hug me. You'd be my friend.
I could talk to you. I could come to you.
You'd teach me things. You'd take me everywhere.
Do you remember? 'Cause I do.
Do you remember the time all the dads came to
play football? And you were the one who scored
the most goals?
I tell people those stories all the time.
Then one day those stories stopped.

One day you became cold. You became impatient,
resentful.
You started to hate me, with no explanation.
Why don't you like me?
What did I do?
Whatever it is I'm sorry.

I need my dad. I need my baba. I need my friend.

I've avoided this conversation for a long time because I didn't want you to see me as weak.
Then I realised it was our fragile conceptions of masculinity that truly make us weak.
We are weak in silence. We are weak alone. We are weak divided.
I'm trying to be strong Baba...

When your dada passed away I could see how broken you were.
I could see the pain. I could see the anger. I could see the regret.
You two never spoke: you shouted... but you never spoke.
You never had a conversation. You didn't know who he was, and he didn't know you.

We don't have to be like that...

Is what I wish I could say to you
If only we could have this conversation.
I just hope you're talking to Dada now.

Kev
by Hannah Tarrington

AMBRA is in a graveyard.

Ambra Amy asked me to marry her. Mad init.

You know, when I talk to you it's like you're in the room with me. I can feel ya, see what you might look like. Floppy ginger curls, sunshine eyes. You're proper muscly too.

You're welcome.

Because we both know there'd be fuck all chance of you getting in a gym if you were here.

It turns me on to think of you like that.

Then I remember that underneath all that soil and mush is a 13-year-old's body and I feel like a right pervert.

This is so fucking stupid.

I've written you a letter, Kev. I, um...

Fuck.

She gets a letter out. She already knows exactly what it says but is clinging to it.

I'm the reason you're dead. Stood there. Useless, did nothing. Watching him. What he did to you. While something broke inside me. It was deeper than the grief of losing a friend. I lost my love. Like, my ability to love. It went. You were my safety blanket, Kev. I used you, squeezed out every bit of comfort I could from you, dragged you to my dad's that weekend cos I was too scared to be there alone, and the world's got a sick fucking sick sense of humour, ain't it, because I have felt lonely and scared ever since.

You know I couldn't come to your funeral: your mum said I was the spawn of Satan. I fantasised about hitting her really hard in the face, just over and over again. Imagined what her bones would sound like crunching against a bat, how warm her blood might feel as it splatted on my face. How satisfying it would be to scream how much of a cunt she was while watching the life drain from her eyes. Then I realised that maybe she wasn't wrong. I swapped her face out for mine and it felt more satisfying.

I was consumed by anger all the time. Until I met Amy. Finally I felt like I could take a breath and the world wouldn't collapse around me. But when she proposed, the first thing I felt was guilt. She's there in front of me, eyes wide, a glimmer of that sunshine that I see in yours, looking at me like I'm home.

All I was thinking about was you. That you would never get a moment like this.

When I said yes you were still in my mind and I couldn't tell if I was saying it to her or you. I've wanted to scream every day since you were murdered. I want to scream right now.

She screams; ends up laughing at herself.

We're not kids running around the estate anymore. You're not real now, you're gone. And I need to let you be gone. You've got my heart but I can't give you my mind too. He can't have my life too.

Goodbye, Kev.

I love you.

Kneel
by Warren Mendy

JAE, a young black man.

Jae   Can't go anywhere now, can you? I've waited
fifteen years to get here, fifteen fucking years!
Went through hell and back! I didn't sleep. I joined
the army. I studied biology just to know exactly
where to shoot you and inflict the slowest, most
painful death you could EVER feel. I trained my
mind and body till every ounce of my being knew its
mission. It was the only way I could live without
him.

Laughs.

No one to teach me how to kick a football, to fix a
plug or shoot hoops. Because you took that from
me. And when you took my dad from me, you also
took my mother. Lost. Addicted. I had to work two
jobs underage just to pay the bills so we wouldn't
get KICKED OUT our one bedroom apartment.
Fifteen year – KNEEL ON THE FLOOR. I SAID
FUCKING KNEEL – fifteen fucking years and now
you kneel before me, begging for your life.

Laughs.

Did you make my dad beg for his before you slaugh-
tered him like a piece of meat? Huuh! Cos you

couldn't stand to see your black friend winning more than you.

It's time for you to go.

Silence. He starts crying as he points the trigger towards the kneeling figure.

I've ached so long for this moment and now I can't even pull the trigger! I thought seeing you beg for your life will make my body bleed out this hate I feel towards you. I thought doing this would – would make me feel human again but it doesn't... It doesn't.

It makes me feel like you. Like nothing.

Leave... leave before I change my mind... leave, leave...

Breaking down.

...I SAID FUCKING LEAVE!

Pulling it all back together – just.

You've killed two of us. That's enough.

Lazy
by Alistair Wilkinson

Rhys   Excuse me?

Take what back?

Take back the fact that I think you are a classist cunt
who's got no fucking idea what real struggle is like?
By you going to me, 'I never said that' or, 'I don't
know where you got that from', you're denying the
truth of what just happened, and excusing your own
behaviour to make it seem like my reaction is silly.
You're trying to make me feel silly.

Nah.

You said it.

I heard it.

I've got ears.

You know I have sat and listened to you make
classist remarks for the last twenty-four hours, and
for some reason I have kept my mouth shut. And
even now I'm pissed off at myself for snapping at
you. Because I'm reacting out of anger, rather than
intellect. And this situation here makes me feel
even more stupid than I usually do, because the
thing is, the working classes are never taught how
to argue – whereas you spoilt pricks get to learn

how to debate from the point you're in fucking nappies.

Seriously, how the fuck can you say that because a parent isn't home-schooling their kids during this lockdown it's because they're lazy and don't care? Who the fuck do you think you are? They're not lazy! They're focusing on putting tea on the table, or keeping the bloody leccy on – on fucking surviving!

You've never had to go without, have you?

...Have you?

Because if you haven't, you'll never know what it's like. If you've never had to want for anything, you'll never fully understand. You'll never know that *this* isn't a choice. I am so well equipped to going without, and living with little money, that my problem is I sometimes forget that not everybody has been forced to live off £50 a week, so they don't really have a clue about what's going on outside their fucking bubble.

When you walk into a room, you don't need to worry about sounding or feeling different. Nobody stares at you, because, well, you're meant to be there.

Ha!

'LAZY'.

Seriously?

You know, next time you even think of opening your mouth to say, 'Oh, there's something they could do – maybe they just don't really want to', think about what *you* could do to help. Like keeping your fuck-ing mouth shut for once.

Let this be beautiful
by Tom Colgan

Elgan   You're lying, Sharon.

You told me you were here to help me get to the truth. 'You and me,' you said, 'we'll work this all out. Together.' We had to be honest with each other if I wanted to get better.

But we weren't, were we?

I mean, I was. I opened up to you, Sharon. Told you things I've never told anyone. Showed you the letter I'd written. Not even my brother got to see that, and it was him who made me come to you in the first place.

I let you examine everything. All the little pieces of my broken brain. So you could put them all together. I thought we were making something beautiful out of me, but instead of bringing me the full picture, you threw it over my head.

Y'know, there are a lot of people who are experts at keeping secrets from me. My brother probably would've kept his gob shut if you'd told him. My dad – well, I don't pay him enough attention to catch wind of anything he knows. But you chose to go to the one person in my life that would slip up. The one person who really struggles to lie to someone's face even when the chips are down.

I think I take after her in that.

Got to give you credit though, Sharon: you're stealthy. I reckon you could quit CAMHS[1] and become a PI if you wanted. But see, my mam, she just lacks the finesse of the practised liar. Didn't even bat an eyelid, let alone clock on when I asked to borrow the laptop to print off my chemistry coursework. Opened it up, and it was right there on the desktop. Big old questionnaire to help you diagnose me as something I had no idea I could possibly be.

She'd started filling it in, too. It's a fascinating read. You'll lap it up. I did. That's why I didn't print my coursework in the end.

No.

I printed that.

And of course the most fucked up thing about this is I've spent three months talking to you about how I never really trust that people are being straight with me. How nobody ever says what they're really feeling, and how that makes it really hard for me to stop wondering if they like me at all. Of course, now I know that's because I'm autistic. This beautiful key to all of my issues and anxieties, everything I didn't

---

[1] *CAMHS: child and adolescent mental health services.*

understand about my brain, the one thing that could have really helped me. But you kept it from me so you could continue observing me. And that casually and cruelly, you not only ruined my trust in you, but you ruined my trust in the woman who I thought would always be there for me.

You made this safe little room into something treacherous and ugly.

And I'm tired of feeling like my whole life is one ugly thing after another.

So I'm going to let this be beautiful.

I'm going to let myself be beautiful.

And I'm never coming back to this hospital again.

Lobster
by Benjamin Salmon

Harry   Two nights ago, I penetrated the poshest twat in the world.

Honestly. The poshest twat you'll ever meet in your life... Posher than the Queen riding a horse on her personal truffle farm. Like, posh. Like, really really posh.

Posh twat's name is Cameron.

Nothing wrong with posh people like Cameron. The way I feel about engaging with posh people is the same as how I feel about eating lobster – it's just not for me.

Posh twat Cameron has been obsessed with me for about two and a half years, and I've spent most of those two and a half years actively avoiding him because although he has the arse of an angel, he refers to rugby as 'the rugger', and that is absolutely the fastest way imaginable to kill my erection.

I used to spend my early twenties quietly reprimanding myself for fancying boys like Cameron who feel they can mansplain everything to me because they were privately educated, but the more sexually frustrated I've become in my twenties I've just simply allowed myself to shag whoever I want and deal with the consequences later, like every other single and emotionally reckless homosexual man I know.

Me penetrating Cameron was somewhat of a surprise because I am the sort of gay man who likes to be penetrated – specifically by lonely fifty-five-year-old men who enjoy being called 'Daddy'. But Cameron isn't fifty something, and instead I want him to call me daddy because I'm absolutely obsessed with his arsehole. It's all quite the turn of events, really.

And actually, once you get past the fact that Cameron talks like a knob, and that his mum is a problematic white South African, and that no matter how nice he is and no matter how hard he wants to understand, he'll never actually truly understand the value of money and why you can't just get Deliveroo at the drop of a hat even if you really really really can't be arsed to cook, and why that means you have to spend weeks and weeks living off packets of Tesco custard creams whilst you hate yourself for not being more conventionally attractive because you truly believe that being the owner of a successful, thriving OnlyFans account could well and truly be the answer to all of your problems... once you sort of just force yourself to accept the disgusting, wrath inducing, depressing, deep rooted imbalance between two people like Cameron and me – that's when you sort of just realise that someone like Cameron is actually quite wonderful.

He's just really lovely. Even with all the posh stuff.

I think I get off on him calling me daddy when we have sex because that's the only way I can feel comfortable in his two bedroom flat in Highgate Village. But also because we have really exciting sex. And I've never found sex to be so exciting. Now it's like someone's turned on the light and I've discovered that it actually doesn't need to be terrifying and overwhelming. And it can just be really fucking... nice.

Posh twat Cameron's my new favourite person, even if his favourite hobby is baking focaccia.

Again – nothing wrong with focaccia. I just can't stand focaccia. But Cameron's focaccia actually tastes quite nice.

Lost Boy
by Aimee Pollock

TINA. Mid to late 20s. Outside a small seaside bar along the White Cliffs of Dover. Late afternoon.

Tina   Thought I'd find you up here. Beautiful view, init? On a clear day, you can see France… Yeah: look.

Twenty-six miles. That's all it takes. To sail away and become someone else entirely.

I'm sorry I pulled away just now, Rob. It's not that I don't like you, it's just… I was at work. I was working.

Attention is just part of my job. I was tryna be nice. Being nice, though, is not an invitation for you to try and kiss me. It's not meant to be anything but good to see you. And it is. Good to see you.

Working in a bar, men come on to me, they're inappropriate with me. And I don't always know how to handle it. It's like, am I being too flirty or too defensive? How do I let my guard down when I constantly feel their eyes burning through my body? What's the right kind of smile? Do I even wanna smile? I feel like a fucking animal trapped inside a cage.

You're not like them.

You don't even look me in the eye.

I can pour a pint and you won't say, 'Fancy giving me more head,' with a wink.

In fact, you remind me of my brother, Luke. Get a couple drinks down ya neck and the words start flowing, but until such time it's like pulling blood from a stone.

I actually like being alone in the bar with you.

Squaddie, right? Staying at the Burstin Hotel?

I always longed to live somewhere else. Literally anywhere else but here. A city. Far, far away from the sea, where no other soul knows who I am, wandering from place to place. Anonymously.

You know that feeling, don't you?

Twenty-seven unidentified male bodies have washed up on this very shore since 1971. Twenty-seven unidentified.

Luke Richardson. 2008. He found it difficult too. Most blokes around here do. Until they've sniffed a few lines and downed a few pints that is. My mum would always say, *they just need to find the right girl and settle down.*

It doesn't work like that.

A few more years, I'm gunna be running this bar. I have to. The grand total of my life, my specialised skill set: knowing quickly and specifically what people like to drink. I can tell how old they are from that, *and* how many drinks it's gunna take for them to piss me off, which nine times outta ten...

Every day, when I see you across the bar

I think about sailing away a little less.

I don't wanna look across the bar

and be

haunted

by the memory of you.

I want to sit at the bar with you. Listening to your mumbled stories about the world six pints in. Or discover it in the books I know you leave behind for me. I wanna hear it all. I can't fix you with a kiss, unfortunately. But I am a woman who's willing to help you unload whatever it is you're carrying around, because I'm telling you now, you ain't gunna find anything worth having down there. We'll both be lost. Do you understand? For good. You can trust me on that.

I think you understand.

Take my hand, Rob.

Walk with me.

Love Language
by Lauren Greer

Lily   Why do they bother teaching us French and Spanish in school, eh?

'Languages will unlock doors for you, for the rest of your life' – what a load of shite that was. The only thing I remember is grassy-ass and that's because Mr. Henning jumped around and slapped his arse when he said it.

Love languages, that's what they should teach in schools. There are five ways of communicating love, did you know that?

Affirmations. Acts of service. Gifts. Spending quality time and physical touch.

You need to know the love language you prefer to give, so that you know who you are; how you're wired to give and receive. And you have to get to know your partner's love language, so you can appreciate what they're trying to do for you, so you can give them what they need. That's it. And that's what I do for Louis.

Nice ring. What's she like, your wife? Do you know her love language?

See, in my house, affirmations sound like, 'I love your fat tits.' And Louis does love me, I know he does, but he shows me love in a way I can't connect to, you know? It's like greasing the pan with hair-

114

spray, yes it's a spray and I asked for it, but it's not the one I need right now.

He bought me a fish. As a gift. A *Finding Nemo* fish. And I... I don't know why. I've never asked for a fish. Do people love fish? As pets? I mean, I love a fish supper but... I thought, what the hell do you do with one that floats around a fishbowl? Don't feed it enough and it dies, feed it too much and it dies, don't let it get too warm or it will die, don't let it get too cold or it'll die. He gave me a gift that was just destined to die. But a ring – *that* wouldn't die. And I'm not saying I wanted a ring, Jesus, I... I... just wanted something that... meant... something.

He works a lot, always does overtime, double shifts, bank holidays, anti-social hours – 'Sure the pay's better,' he says. Muggins here would make big batches of dinner, then freeze a few for him to re-heat when he gets home. 'The best way to a man's heart is through his gut,' me mum always says. But, see, I didn't know his heart was already full up. And his balls were being emptied by...

So he's packing his bags and I'm screaming at him, and he just continues in silence. Silently folding his clothes, folding them calmly like I'm not even there. I want him to look at me, to touch me, tell me it's another one of his shit pranks, but he doesn't. So I block the bedroom door – I don't want him to leave me. He pushes me, really hard, and I fall back. And then we're both pulling this fucking fishbowl and it... it just flew, so fast, and it smashed, and Nemo was flopping furiously on the ground – and then he dropped like a sack of spuds, there was blood pissing out of his head, and I panicked. I could see Nemo's flopping was slowing down and I knew he was dying, I had to save him.

He didn't deserve this, he was totally innocent, but he was trying to take him away from me. Nemo was my fish: he bought him, but he was mine, he was bought for me, and I was so scared he was gonna die... So yes, I suppose I did, hit, him.

Love Me Or Die
by Josie White

Shaughna   I thought about what you said the other day. You know, about me being scared of people and that's why I push them away. But I think you're wrong. I'm not scared of people. I hate them. I hate them because I can't connect with them. I don't feel anything for them. Like, last week I went to my grandfather's funeral. I made sure I sat on the front row of the church and I stared at the coffin for the entire service, just praying I'd feel something. Anything... And then the strangest thing happened. All of a sudden all I could think about, all I could feel... was you. You made me feel something. And I can't quite put my finger on what it was. All I know is that for the first time, in a long time, I feel something. I... I feel love... I think I love you. And that's so amazing because you know more than anyone that most days, most of the time, actually, I feel nothing. I watch a sad film – I don't cry. I see a homeless person on the street – I don't feel sorry for them. I think of all the fucking injustices the common folk like me have to put up with – I don't feel angry. Does that make me evil?

And now I've had, what, six sessions with you? And you've decided that I've made next to no progress and you've given up on me. Oh, sorry, not given up, you 'think I'd get more effective results working with another professional.' You've decided I'm a monster. That I'm beyond help. Well, how do you think that makes me feel? I know I struggle with the whole 'feelings' thing, but I do almost get a little twinge of something sometimes... Like, for instance, right now I feel the impulse to take some sort of shiny, sharp object and just slowly drive it right through your fucking eye. To watch you feel every nerve popping, every vein exploding, every blood vessel bursting, until all you see is nothing...

I'm obviously not going to do that, I'm not a psycho. But I do think that it's true what they say, that it's a fine line between love and hate. Or maybe they're just the same thing and neither feeling is real.

I guess what I'm trying to say is... I love you... But if you ever try and walk away from me again, that'll be your last day with legs.

Ninety-Six
by Christie Reynolds

ALANNAH, Liverpudlian accent.

Alannah   Abar a hundred did you say? Is that how many people you think there was? Is that what the chat was the next morning in the break-room was it? 'Abar a hundred people.'

Beat.

There was 96.

Ninety fucking six, and they wer't even just men and women. Some of them were fucking kids. Dragged out onto the pitch. Families queueing up outside a sports hall waiting to go in and scour the rows of bodies, praying to god that the tiny footy boots of the kid in the back corner weren't too familiar. Not their babies. Because how could that be true? How do people go off to watch the footy one Saturday and not come home? How? No, am asking ye 'ere, come on, how? Because that just doesn't make sense in my head.

Who's at fault? Who's to blame here? Cos I don't think it's us. The scousers. The 'pickpockets'. The 'scumbags'.

But that's what you wanna convince everyone, isn't it? 'Get it in the paper! Get it on the news! Make them the target so people don't start pointing fingers at us' – the ones who make the building regulations and cut the corners that cost lives. Who own the stadiums and the newspapers. We're not fuckin' stupid. It's an old trick. Blaming the people at the bottom. Leaving us to fight amongst each other like rats so that people – people like you, poxy posh journalists, with yer bloody big briefcase and yer nice suit – get off scot-free. Thinking you're better than us cos ye talk nice. Cos your ma can afford to spend more on her knickers than mine can spend on leccy.

I don't know how you sleep at night. Knowing the truth, that it wasn't our fault. KNOWING that it wasn't the dads putting their kids on their shoulders to get them over the crowds. Or the people forming human fuckin' chains to pull their mates up from the stands below them, and it certainly wasn't the mums queueing up outside a sports hall. So what are we gonna do? Because there's ninety-six people dead 'ere, and that blood is on your hands.

Not Compatible With Life
by Nieve Hearity

Abby Is this a joke?

Please tell me this is a joke.

Please.

Wait, no, stop.

Start again, what do you mean? What is anenceph-aly?

Genetic condition? But – not compatible with life? Not compatible? He's not a phone with the wrong charger he's a baby, he's my baby!

There must be something you can do, I've seen those documentaries, you can do anything these days. I saw one, they operated on the baby while it was still in the womb, it was a little girl and they operated on her, they took her out and fixed her then they put her back in and she was fine, she was born and she was fine and healthy and they fixed her! Can't you do that? Can't you fix him?

No, you don't understand!

I'm going to breastfeed. I read a study that children who breastfeed have better immune systems and do better in school. His dad's got sensitive skin, haven't you, Jai? He might have it too; I've been saving up for the John Lewis sleep suits coz they're softer. We've decorated his room – blue walls and

white clouds. We had a fight over buying his pram!
We've picked his nursery and his school. Jai's got
him a   little football kit!

Listen! Please just listen to me. He's got a name.
Alexander James Porter. He's already here, he's
already a person. You can't say he's not compatible
with life. I feel him moving, I feel him kicking, he's
alive in me.

Pause.

What can we do?

I'm six months gone; I can't do that. You telling me
to kill him then give birth to him. How do I go into
hospital and give birth to my son then just leave
him there? Please, please don't ask me to.

Beat.

I've miscarried four times.

We've done the tests, we've done all the fertility
treatments, we've done everything you told us to.
He's the only one I carried past the first trimester.
We're so close, please, there must be something.

Silence. Looks down at her bump and cradles it.

I'm sorry we did this to you, Alex. I wish I could keep
you in here where it's safe. We want you so much.

I keep thinking about Christmas, I see the tree and
the decorations, you're sleeping in my arms and I'm

having a cheeky glass of prosecco while the family is there talking and laughing and I'm looking at you and feeling so happy, so complete.

I've got you a baby Santa suit, it's a bit big but you'll be a few months old by then.

 Would have been.

I would have been a good mum. I'd have been strict, but always listen, understand, support you no matter who you grew up to be. I've imagined your whole life, your first word, your first steps, walks in the park, your hand in mine. Your first day at school, at uni… I never imagined this.

I'm proud of you. You tried so, so hard to be here. You did your best, son.

Mummy and Daddy love you so much.

Night night, sleep tight.

Our Last Adventure
by Charis McRoberts

Aoife   This is it then. Time to say bye-byes. Sorry there's
no one else. Auntie Lynn had work and Da couldn't
be arsed. Serves you right though, Nanny. You were
an oul bitch, weren't ya? Nasty piece of work.
Shouldn't be telling you this really but I reckon you
know – that Mammy never liked ye. That whole
'you stole my son' business. She played 'Ding Dong
The Witch Is Dead' the day after we found ya. That's
a great honour, you know. I bet you're living it up
down there, arm in arm with Maggie T herself. Ma
swears blind it was a coincidence, that it just
'popped up' on Spotify. I'm not so sure. Da certainly
didn't think it was funny. I'm proper pissed off
about it all. Talk about inconvenience. I'll have to
buy me own sweets now. And what will I do with
my Tuesday afternoons? How will I get me five
pounds a week to spend at the shops? You could
have tried to stick around a little longer, until I'd
finished school at least and escaped this shite hole.
Now I can't use you as an excuse when I want to go
over to Eoin's. You know it's my birthday next week
as well. Could you not have waited until after the
party? It'll be no fun now Mammy's got no one to
argue with.

Da says I have to get a job now too. Says I'll be old
enough and don't have you to look after. Even

though it was always more you looking after me. Anyways, I can't be fucked. I've more important things to be doing than packing shopping bags or walking dogs. Don't be asking what, though, 'cause that's none of your business, is it?

Toby had to be put in a shelter. I'm sorry. I tried me best but Da wouldn't let me keep him. I had this grand plan to hide him at Eoin's but he shat all over their white living room carpet. His mum went mad. I near pissed myself it was so funny. You would have loved it. I really miss our Toby. And I really really miss you, nanny.

Right. Enough of that. To business.

Aoife stands, lifting the urn.

What am I meant to do with you anyway? Sprinkle ya or throw ya? Hm, don't want you to get caught in the wind and blow back in my face. Gross. Can you imagine? Right then, pour ya it is.

On the Lagan you float with no boat. Your final adventure taking you to the afterlife, our last adventure together.

Night Nanny, sleep tight.

Pavement Boss Man
by Aoife Smyth

Muggins *(Belly laugh.)* Mate?

Mate
The audacity
Of you
Rocking up to me
In trainers
Nicer than mine
Asking me
If I've got a spare cigarette
Who's got a spare cigarette?
I dunno about any of the other poor fuckers you con on the regular
but when I bought this pack of Sterling Dual
and am taxed out of my arsehole at eleven pound a pop
I fully intend on smoking each and every one of these 20 death sticks myself
And plan on doing so uninterrupted by a pavement boss man in brand new Nike Airs
Nah where you going?
We're mates now apparently so let's talk about it
Nah you came over to me so let's talk about it
Let's say I gave you a ciggie now yeah
I'm not fucking gonna but if I did
and I were to divide this pack of 20 by 11,
we're looking at about 55p a pop
For one

For two

How do I know you're not collecting them?

Yeah

Stashing them away

In empty packs

Selling em off

Like a gretty pick n mix

Making a killing doing so

While muggins over here

Slaves over

Whatever job I'm doing at the time to keep myself
afloat

And I come out the tube

Death warmed up

On my way to the bus stop

Daily

And I see you

Daily

Lingering about Stratford station

With an estimated footfall of around

Fuck knows

Tens

Of thousands of people a day

Knowing

That if I did that

Full time

Collecting cigarettes

From poor passers by

I could quit my job

Tell Gina at work to fuck off
Not have to worry about Benjamin fucking Price
nicking my coffee mug every day and pretending it
weren't him
Crack of dawn
Staring myself dead in the eyes in
The mirror I'm too knackered to clean
Wondering how I got here

Nah
I could work for myself
Outside Stratford station
Take as many fag breaks as I want
Tell you what
You're onto a winner here pavement boss man
Got any jobs going?

Peace in this hoose
by Sarah Ord

Isla   I know that I'm a nightmare. I know that my
demons circle above oor heeds as we sleep at opposite sides o the bed. I know that my lack o love
and affection has sent us in opposite directions. I
know this –

I can see your throat is on fire, flames are shooting
oot yoor skull as I stand here staring straight
through ya. My eyes are deid, like an abandoned
haunted hoose in the middle of a burnt doon forest.
Niver once have I managed to look at you straight in
the eye. Fucking coward. I thought that if we iver
locked eyes that all the betrayals would come leak-
ing oot my sockets and spill onto the fleer in front o
me, reflecting back the true arsehole that I really
am.

I tell him he has to go. I have packed up his shite car
and he is going. I have had enough of his crap, I say.
I am wanting a fresh start for my aching heart and
staying here with him just fills me we dread.

Fuck me. Even in oor final goodbyes I cana muster
up the courage to tell the poor man the proper
truth. I hiv spilled oot so many lies from my lips that
I cana even fathom fit the truth is onymare.

Over the years I have broken him. No doot about it.
Each lie like a boulder crashing through his caravan

of love. Smashing him up one lie at a time. All that remains of him noo is a skeleton o the structure that once stood in this neighbourhood of young desire.

I told him that I wiz workin late. I told him that I wiz doing an exercise class online. I told him I was having a freen roon for a glass of vino so that he needed to scarper. I told him my family were visiting for the night and they needed the double bed. I told him I wiz hosting an Avon party and having drinks wee the quines. I told him onything that would get him off my bloody back and oot the hoose for a few hours.

It's pathetic. But it's the only thing that silences the voices in my heed. The only thing that calms me doon and make me feel relaxed again. It's the only thing that lets me escape the mundane monotony of life and make me feel excited and alive. Christ! It's the only thing that makes me feel fucking happy!

So here I am, tonight I am up to my old ways. He throws doon his hoose keys on the nest o table and slams the front door. As far as he is concerned, we are over.

Breathes.

Love Island Season 7 starts tonight in 20 minutes.

Dinna worry – I'm nae completely heartless – I

already saved my grovelling text tae my drafts summarising my love and adoration, ready to ping it over to him in the last ad break.

He should get it just before he reaches the first service station.

Breathes.

Fucking peace at last.

Proud
by Lekhani Chirwa

ALICIA, Northerner, 18-22 years old.

Alicia   Why do you hate me? Go on. You can say it. I can take it.

I *can* handle it. Whatever it is that you're holding in. Let it out! Is it resentment? What did I do to make you treat me this way? Every time I come home it's some snide remark about my accent or my style or which fucking alcoholic beverage I choose. Like why does any of that even matter?

You can't stand it, can you? You can't stand that I got out and made something of myself. But it's like you don't want me to succeed. Do you know what, it's pathetic. Just because *you're* so fucking complacent and docile, you can't be happy for anyone else. You never stop complaining but you never do anything about it. You'll never admit that, though, will you? You'll never actually just be fucking honest and fucking real with yourself about the choices *you* made. Or didn't make. And I try with you. I *really* fucking *try* and you give me nothing.

And I miss you. I admit it. I miss you, Shaz.

I thought moving to a new place, starting from scratch would be an adventure. Like if nobody knew me, then I was free to be anyone I wanted. But mostly I'm just lonely.

When the group chats pop up with updates of baby-showers and christenings that I'm not invited to. I read all the in-jokes and new banter and it's like a foreign language. I don't know what to say, so I don't say anything, and then I feel ignored. Like a ghost. You've all cried at my funeral, given me a send-off and now you've moved on.

What I want so badly to do is share and celebrate where I'm at, how far I've come. Have a good old laugh with my family and friends about the ridiculously priced London drinks, the house-share dramas and the countless times I've gotten lost. But the girls straight up refuse to come down to visit. All they care about is the next piss-up holiday to bloody shagaluf! I mean, like, yes it's expensive down here but no more than going abroad.

And how do you think it makes me feel to be told I'm too posh now? Yeah, I know you say it's jokes, but that shit hurts. 'Cause I can tell you now that down here I am not fucking posh. I try to speak proper 'cause I *have* to. To get to where I wanna go I *have* to put on an act. I *have* to try and fit in. But no one's fooled. And when I think to myself at least I can come home where I belong, you lot push me away.

There's been times where I've really needed you.

Shit has hit the fan on numerous occasions and I call and call and call. No response.

You see, it's not about what you do, it's what you don't do. You never ask how things are going. Never congratulate me. Never comfort me. We used to do that. Have each other's back and it was two fingers to everyone else. We always had us. No one makes me laugh like you, Shaz. No one is as funny or as brave or as honest as… you as you are. And I get that you don't understand me anymore and maybe, yeah, I don't totally understand you.

But I do want you to be proud of me.

Like I'm proud of you.

Puppy Pound
by Sam Purkis

*MARCUS has broken into Battersea Dogs Home. He's
watching a golden retriever lick itself.*

Marcus Hello boy. Or is it girl? I can't see your genitals from
here in the torchlight. Wanna come with me? I've
got plenty of chow and even those sticks you chew
so your breath doesn't smell like the plague. Yes,
life's been ugly for you, but you're still beautiful.

Our first pet is the perfect metaphor for a family,
our health, our collective behavior mirrored back at
us in lupine form, its lifeforce enhanced or inhibited
by us. Pets reflect our natural love, bond and community. They cower when we teach them to fear,
they fight when we teach them conflict and they kill
when we teach them hate. They show us who we
are.

My first dog Charlie was (and I know this is cliché)
my best friend. We got him just before I was born,
you could even say he got me but I don't wanna
sound like a cunt. We grew up together, both
starting so small, but I remember watching as he
transformed from this vessel of play and affection
to this snarling, foolhardy splinter of violence. It was
mainly to protect, of course. It was still devastating
to see his devolution. I remember the first time this
kindling ignited in rageous fury; we were in the

countryside, the day was just golden, that's the only way I can describe it. I still felt the loving gaze of my mum then too. Sun from all sides. Charlie was running around the bullpen again, taunting the big buggers (or playing with them: it became hard to tell) and this horrible abusive bastard – the kind you hope doesn't have kids – kicks off at us for blocking some mud path, getting aggressive towards Mum, cane flying everywhere. His English bull terrier snapped at Charlie, then towards me, and I just waited. Calmly observed how my darling boy tore the other dog's ear off, the terror in its physicality, the man flailing and hitting.

Watching Charlie was dread-inducing but exhilarating, like when you're a kid and the attendant pulls your seat-lock down before you're launched out of the latest rollercoaster that feels like it's used to test out future train models on kids at theme parks, the collateral damage...

Or maybe I'm just fully tapped now, and that's the thing about insanity: when you're in here it's the same as being sane. Look at me, looking at everything. Analysing every detail. I'm feeling a bit analytical, aren't I? Lyrically anal. Fucking Sigmund Freud. Overthinking. Over complicating. I could've just said, 'Like the ending of *Inception*,' and you'd've probably got it.

The man was spinning. His fury becoming fear like a

mime changes face, eventually retreating with half
the calf muscle he stepped out with and a half-dead
man's best friend.

That's probably when I changed. I thought, 'Karma
ain't a cunt when a cunt gets karma.'

Look at you. Tongue hanging, tail wagging. Just the
right amount of dopey. Come on, before the alarm
calls the blue jumper lot to come and catch us. Let's
get you the fuck out of here.

Radical Temptation
by James G. Nunn

Lucifer I know it wasn't me you were calling. But he doesn't hear you, he won't listen to you. Why would he? He created this world that has put you on your knees. he chose the kings who live in luxury paid for by your poverty. The souls of a once proud people, crushed and grounded to fertilise their garden.

But I hear you! I am with you at your lowest, when you have given everything and have nothing left. I am that warming hug of hate, the sweet kiss of anger, that soothing fantasy of revenge. What has his patience and tolerance brought you? Nothing but misery and destitution. Put your faith in me. I can give you the power and dignity you deserve – now!

Let me course through your veins and harden your heart. I will take away your pain, I will burn up your fear, I will take your screams of dying dreams and tear down your enemies. No longer will you be under the cosh of the kings, you will hold it!

Get off your knees, bow to no one, no king, no queen, no prince, no priest, no power, no god! Stand! Your head up, shoulders back, fists clenched, tall and proud, for now the world looks to you. This world that tempted you with ambitions and dreams of success, then chewed you up? Well, we will make it choke! Together we will slash the throat of society, cut the bonds of civility and remake this world in our image.

And what shall we do with the kings? Those who have the most yet are given more, those that control the most yet are given more control, and those who set the rules of the game they have already cheated? We must treat them with the same contempt they have shown for us. No more compliance, No more cooperation, just rebellion and chaos!

You are the reckoning, you are the maggot in their feast, the shit on their shoe, the spit in their champagne. We will make them pay in their blood for what they took with ours. Let ME in and you won't need anyone to listen to you anymore: WE will make them hear!

Rouge
by Rachelle Coffie

STEPH, a mixed race black woman, holds a cigarette in bloody hands. She inhales.

Steph I lost myself. In denial about what was and what could have been. I wanted to feel nothing, just like you. I want to feel nothing, just like you. I saw when you did. You tapped out! Fuck! I prepared myself for if I ever had your kid. I lost myself. Thank fuck we never did. Think with logic not emotion, right?

Picks up a bottle.

Every time you linked Captain Morgan on your raving nights,

Throws it.

Every time you hurled your empty bottles, exploding glass across our walls,
It was you I could see breaking. Projecting your hurt onto my being.
Growing so aggressive even your boys stepped back, stepped away.
Spending all my time picking up your pieces when I couldn't even pick up my own damn pieces. *(Stubs out cigarette.)* For once, J, I felt understood. I didn't feel like a trophy to a black brother or having to explain to a grey why I'm not screaming 'All Lives Matter' when right now black lives matter.

What about this life?
This life matters.

Steph bends down to Jordan's level.

Every time I'd start a protest
I'd get abducted by your eyes. The weight of your
head clasped in my hand on my chest. The embrace
of safety. I denied this phenomenon was infatua-
tion, but my people saw me falling. I'm a hard nut
to crack, tough gyal, invincible, but for you, eventually, I let go of alla that. My first inhalation of
vulnerability, the addiction to being wanted. By you.
But I was the 'mixed black girl'. Outspoken. You
couldn't handle that. I fell in mad love with someone who wouldn't love me back. Couldn't love me
back and I'll hold a 'L' for that.

Stands and makes a call.

Hey.
It's me.
That favour you offered if I ever needed? I need it.
Everything. No trace. Dead weight. Gone. Say no
more. Love.

Hangs up.

All I ever asked for was you to tell me how you feel.
It ain't too late. To say what you got to say.

Silence.

Oh, yeah.

Chuckles.

> Till this day you can't be a man still.
> Well, I can be a woman.
> Understand this, I am a fire that can't be tamed. I'm the baddest.

Looks down at hands.

> And now finally I am free.

Rough on Smooth
by Sam Purkis

*CALLUM is at dinner with his new boyfriend Shane's family.
They are posh, Callum is not. He overhears Shane's dad calling
their relationship a phase.*

Callum I respect you being protective over your son, but
you don't have to be such a cunt about it. I'm not
gonna sit here and pretend Shane and I mix in the
same circles. He was in boarding school, whilst I was
sleeping in boarded-up houses. I'm not trying to
pretend I'm some preppy uni boy misusing Latin
and banging on about their dad's businesses in
place of a personality or an original anecdote. I'm
scum by your book, I get it. And I quite like it, to be
honest. Makes me sound like Billy the Kid.

We do have lots in common: we both love your son,
though only I've got the bollocks to tell him that.
You watch *Downton Abbey* which is just *EastEnders*
for Tories. Posh people love their drugs, and I used
to love selling them to youse. You all love a little
Friday afternoon sniff before a pub crawl which
eventually becomes a regular weekly package. I've
bankrupted as many of your lot as you have mine.
You use 'a bit of rough' like it's an insult. Your son
likes my rough. Your sons always do. And your
daughters. Even your wives too, but you chappie
types choose to be less aware of that. Think about

every dirty act you've thought about doing with your secretary. That's what your sons and daughters think about us, about me. I understand you being scared, I'd be scared shitless of me. We work heavy manual jobs. Sculpting us and giving us primate strength. The day you decide to get violent you'll lose and you know it. That's why your style is so passive aggressive, cos ours is anything but.

Don't fret. I don't need to hurt you, I don't want to be you. I want to be better. Look better. Fuck better. Live better. I want to keep close to my community, my music and my laughter. Not this crystallised, Catholicised misery. Yeah, I love him. I'm gonna keep loving him. It's like a sliver of moonlight choosing you, you can see it even in darkness. He loves me and how he leaves smelling of life whenever we've been together. The dirt excites him and my hands are fucking filthy. Yep, that's what you've been smelling on him. Round your house. My hormones. My musk.

Me, when I get home it's a nice long shower. Wash you off. Wank you away. Anyway, nice meeting you, have a good night yeah? Till next time.

RUN DOG BARK
by Alexander Da Fonseca

LEE, any gender. Substitute the word 'lad' in Maxine's dialogue to best suit the performer speaking.

Lee   I think my mum was the most switched on. Which is saying something. She lives in a flat with two dogs – one room, just her (and the dogs) – Tower Hamlets, and her partner in and out all the time. Maxine's like me. But they've got it going on, you know, that's their thing.

They take them on walks together.

They fit. They fit one another. And I never had anyone like that. You tell yourself stories. I mean, we do. Over a night, someone new and they're like this golden glow of 'together'.

And then you wake up. And here's that other feeling.

It's not difficult to charge for it. When you get that feeling. Once you know how.

Probably once in a month, after a long one, up till about twenty, twenty-one, I'd get the first tube in the morning, go and see her. She let me stay. It wasn't that I had nowhere to go – I could've slept over at any of these blokes' – and it was always blokes – easy, no problem. But it was pride I think that made me come back, pride in her having raised me. Just like it was shame that kept me away. Kept me silent whenever I was there. Maxine would always put up a fuss. 'Independent kid like you should be out making a living' – but I knew she grew up down the Peabody flats, and she knew I knew she had some idea of what it was I did.

And the money was really good. Really really good. The kind that means you can't say no.

When I felt most guilty I used to leave some on her bedside. If I couldn't afford it, sometimes I'd just leave mini-rolls. Left her a pack of lightbulbs once, when the power blew. I think she preferred the mini-rolls.

When I got dinged by he who shall remain nameless and the bones in my leg got crushed by his wheel it was Maxine who suggested I stay. Mum basically slept the whole time and I'd have tried escaping if Max didn't pin us together under the blanket. Burned through the whole playbook trying to lie my way out of that one. 'Leg needs exercise, GP visit, new girlfriend,' blah. But she saw straight through me.

I'd sleep, wake up side by side, do it again: whole

week went by in that bed. Couldn't touch her. Worst thing is Maxine knew. By that time my leg had healed and Mum was worse. It showed in her skin. You could see the light shining through her if you looked right. She was ugly. I don't think anybody bothered lying to her at that point. She'd stopped taking the dogs out. Then one day we were both better. We still don't speak about it. The dogs are still fat though.

I do wonder what we'd've said.

I told Maxine 'thank you' and said I'd be back on the straight and narrow. She gave me a backpack and said it would make a nice change. She winked. I think she would've kissed me if I'd let her. Before I left she made me promise to come back. Bring something nice.

She probably was just thinking about the dogs.

Everything's got a right to be looked after. If it can love, it deserves love. I know that much. I own that. Enough to be sorry.

I didn't say that though. That would've been good.

Seahorse
by Sarah Ord

Heidi I must've been smoking hot noo. Like some munter of a duckling who transformed intae this shining bright Greek statue, we boobs o a god and flowing river-like hair. And believe me, no one was mare shocked than I wiz.

Fuck. Beauty really is power.

I am standing in a shite bar in my hometoon we one o the biggest pricks from my school that I've nae seen in donkey's years fight for my love and attention. Ye literally canna mak this shit up. I hae a quick scan aroon the shit-hole o a club to see if there was a gaggle o quines in the corner pissing their pants at this 'humiliating prank' they thought they where playin oot. Nithin.

Aright – weird.

He must've had some sort o an agenda. I mean, it was only a mere six years ago he was chuckin Polos off ma heid in the school canteen and chanting 'Hill-Billy Heidi' whenever I walked past.

Fits changed?

The once Golden Boy o school – the funniest fucker, the top shagger, the legend o the pitch and pool – was pissed oot his nut and declaring his desires tae ME while Gerry Cinnamon's 'Belter' pumps oot the stereo. (I'd be lying if I said I wizna half enjoying the potency o his perfume so close to my face.) But fuck, it's a tragedy…

He whipped off his backwards cap and placed it on the bar.

Fits's the catch? He's a full blown Baldy Eagle noo, that's fit. Proper Thin Lizzy on top. I mean, to put it into perspective, I currently hae mare hair growing oot my left oxter than he has on his heed (and I shaved this morning)…

He used to hae this lush locks o midnight dark hair that he'd flick oot his eyes when he walked doon the corridors, made him all mysterious and dam-aged looking – the Italian Stallion o Aiberdeen people use to call him. But noo? He looked mare like a seahorse! He had a smooth tongue and a smooth heid and there was nae chance I was going for a ride on that een.

Dina get me wrong. I was quite likin this lang over-due social acceptance. Started imagining fit it might be like to procreate with the top fish of oor school, haying thousands o tiny wee fry babies – mating for life.

We would laugh at how we where once star-crossed lovers that the world just couldn't quite handle yet. Beautiful. His freens would gasp in horror as they saw us glide hand and hand doon the street with their main man – hoping and praying that these unborn babies turned oot nithin like their socially inept mither.

But ye see, seahorses are just trophies. They are abducted from the ocean and left to bake in the boiling sun before being sold as souvenirs. This baldy stud hung around the necks o half the girls in this toon and was clearly running oot of buyers noo. He obviously saw me as an easy customer. Gads. Nah, nae for me thanks.

I dooned my last drink and gave him my number – the wrong one. Obviously. Needless to say he clearly thought it went swimmingly as he high-fived his chum on the way to the bog.

Dickhead.

In a flood o rage I whipped oot my pack o Polos from my handbag and launched one at his heed.

Bullseye.

Right on the noggin.

Sent to Cov
by Tom Wright

Ashley When we visit *his* family in the West Country we
indulge in ambles across the misty moors, sightings
of wild ponies and scrumptious scones drenched in
Devonshire cream and homemade jam. Cream first.

In return, my boyfriend gets a claustrophobic city-
scape of construction works almost entirely engulf-
ing Coventry's *two* majestic cathedrals. We sneak
just a peak of the saucy Lady Godiva statue before I
deceptively cut behind the Transport Museum to
avoid introducing bae to West Orchards Stabbing
Centre.

Ah! The Belgrade Theatre – refuge of my youth –
with its majestic fountain, that some clever cunt's
put washing up liquid into. Again. Detour hastily
along *medieval* Spon Street, glide past *Europe's biggest* Ikea and finish in the luscious, greenish embrace of the Memorial Park for a scallop and
ketchup batch. My formerly unwilling feller's subtle
half-moon grin tells me I might have just gotten
away with it.

Legs weary, we decide to brave the cramped top
floor of the number 13 bus over to Mum's. We're
engrossed in sharing hilariously tragic childhood
memories when I clock a group of familiar boister-
ous man-boys boarding our bus. Their bellowing

banter bombarding upstairs, breaching our rom-com return.

'Wagwan fam.' I feel the body next to mine tense up immediately, as boyfie shits himself. 'Big shot made it back to ends then, yeah?' 'Is bin time bruv. Was the crack?' I shudder, then, without hesitation, I transform. 'Yeaaaah boy! Visiting my mum's yard, ennit. Nuff vibes coming back to Cov though, still. Y'get me? Truss.'

I hate myself. My beloved twists his flawless, wholly moisturised body so far into the grubby window that mandem don't even ask who I'm lipsin. It's only as we both vacate, reluctantly in tandem, they shout: 'Still doin batty boy tings then, yeah? Wasteman.'

We march through Mum's estate in stoic silence. The familiar fear triggering the return of darker memories: snowballs filled with rocks; roaming fists exploding through science class windows; loaded 'poof's shot like bullets; a wide-built balaclava fig-ure positioned outside the one-in-a-town sticky-floored gay bar, sparing me his shank only cause he 'knows my older brother, ennit.' Spudding me like we're tight. Programming my mind with tricks to survive. Protect myself. Perform.

But that act ain't needed now. Outdated hormones lurking in my bloodstream, still. Coagulating un-healthily. Stopping me from ever truly being part of his 'middle England'. He's gonna ghost me and go home. I can feel it. This ain't his world. Fuck it.

'This is I me,' I declare on a grassy mound outside Mum's yard, youts playing nearby, and all neighborhood eyes on us. 'The good, the bad... and the Coventry.'

My dazzling guy giggles and brings his mouth in close to my ear. 'I'm into it.'

SH*T
by Becky Lennon

SALLY is sat on a hilltop, looking up.

Sally   Shit. It's the one thing that unites us all. We all shit. Granted not always out ya arse but if it goes in it must come out, somehow. Well, shit needs to be cleaned away. But whose job's that? Some people clean their own shit and get on with their day. Whereas others shit and someone else does it for 'em. So, basically I'm a professional shit shoveller. A shit shifter. I clean posh people's poo, so its fancy shit. Ooh-la-la loos and class A crap. And I don't mind it, yano, cleaning other people's shit.

Anyways, I've just been on a date, well nah, a few hours ago. It started off proper well, he met me off the bus outside Co-op, and we went to this fancy Italian that had bread on the table. Mega polite and all that. He smiled a lot. Propa nice smile – definitely had train tracks when he was younger: they are not natural gnashers – and we had a good laugh and a giggle. I was thinking, 'Yeah, this is alright. He's bearable, not a complete twat like what I used to mess around with, maybe a second date's on the card 'ere.' Then he asked what I did, I told him and he laughed at me. And I'm not talking the type of laugh we've both been passing back and forth to one another. Nah, this laugh was like a, 'Ha, what?

you serious?' type of laugh. Like, what the fuck. Why was he laughing for? Is it funny that I choose to clean other people's shit? Does that make me any less than him? I chose this job, because I'm a) fucking good at it, 2) I enjoy it and d) urm... It's not easy, and I work friken hard. Just as hard – actually no: harder – than him in his pretty suit pushing calculator buttons all day. Pfft, anyways, I left. Had a good night at the pub, so fuck him, I don't need a man anyway. You did just fine on your tod and I turned out alright, din I.

So yeah, I thought I'd come see you. It's been too long, and a miss ya. I know I've not been the best, but it's hard. Growing up and all that, finding my feet. I thought you would be proud of me – doing something good with ma life, instead of being stuck in a dead-end job like you made me promise I wouldn't do. And I own me own business now. Yeah, you 'eard right, your Sal now owns an actual fucking business! I started off cleaning a couple of houses on me own and now I have a little team of gals that work for me, so not only am I a shit shoveller myself, I employ others to shit-shovel for me! It's really profesh!

Yep! Cheers to me – and you, Mam. Done it on our own, din't we! And I promise I won't leave it as long next time, alright? And next time I'll bring flowers and weed killer. And one day we'll get you a new stone. Alright? You deserve it.

Toasts a tinnie in the air.

To owning our business! The shit shovellers! To us!

Shoot Your Load and Go
by Vicky Wild

Kelly   Ee-arr, mop yourself up with that. *(Beat.)* Thanks for the opportunity. It's not everyday someone like me gets to be pleasured by a wanker banker – banker wanker – whichever way round it is. Ooh, that caught your attention. Yer know what I mean... Guess yer not all wankers. Well, you are in one respect. Sorry, I'll stop saying it now. To be honest, it's just an easy word to rhyme it with. But you fingering me in that lift then going down on me too, I'll never forget that. You've got a real talent there. Had me in all sorts of positions. One point it felt like I was flying. Talk about a workout, who needs the gym, eh, when they've got you? And if it weren't for the app I doubt our paths would've ever crossed otherwise.

Lucky you, eh? And lucky me. I can add yer to my list now. Call me sentimental but I like to keep a record. So I can look back when I'm grey and old and think, yeh, I did him and him and him – you get the idea – and it felt bloody good. I'm proud of this one. Don't understand why so many girls carry all this shame around, like you've got to keep your total number on the down low or something. For me, every time is a win. Someone wanted me enough to come round and shoot their load.

Don't worry, I know you're not for keeps, it was just a one-night sorta thing. I ain't one to pester.

You falling asleep? Men after sex, eh. Shot your load, now yer need your little rest. Bless. Right, come on, sweetie pie, up you get. Get yer pants back on. You gonna need to get going, I've got to put a wash on, sort myself out an' that for tomorrow. Can't have you getting attached now, can we?

Eh, hang on, I'll have less of that! Cheeky bastard. 'Stupid slag' my arse. Says he who's doing his buttons up wrong, looking a right state. I'm studying for my A-level maths actually, along with a couple of other subjects. No, I'm not underage or anything, I'm just doing them late. Did a BTEC in Hair & Beauty before, but it just weren't me. Got pushed into it by school, but I was just a bit shit at it. No one ever mentioned university, let alone Oxford or Cambridge. For us it was straight into work, hard graft, making sure we don't all sign on and get knocked up by some bloke – our expectations were manipulated and managed. Bet it weren't like that wherever you went.

Oh yeah? Get you! Bet Mummy and Daddy were proud.

I know, I know, I'm not taking anything away from you, I'm sure you worked very hard. But so did I. I loved Maths. Got top marks in every test before Mum hit the bottle. Then other things sorta took over really. Mitigating circumstances, you could call it. Then she died. Took an overdose. It were me what found her.

Nah, don't say sorry. You don't mean it. And that's alright. But I'd love to do what you do. Honestly. Do you think I could give it a shot myself? *(Beat.)* Really? You'll say anything to get another shag and a kip. But thanks. And you know what? I'm gonna do it. I'm gonna be a wanker banker.

Split the Bill
by Tricia Wey

Words in square brackets [] should be said out loud but indicate the character's inner thoughts.

DANNY sits on a chair, reading a menu.

Danny [Shit.]

> *(To audience.)* I knew this place was gonna be expensive, but it's even more than I thought.
>
> I can't afford this bougie kind of stuff; I mean, £15 for a bowl of soup? As a starter? I can get three tins of Heinz for a pound down the offie.
>
> My mind starts racing with excuses, trying to land on one that actually sounds believable.
>
> Already got dinner at home?
>
> Ate a big lunch?
>
> Fasting for Lent?
>
> When even is Lent? Is now the right time for Lent?
>
> Deep breath. *(To table.)* Sorry guys, I've gotta go. Yeah, yeah, I know it's early but there's actually… closures on the Victoria line, so I've gotta go some mental way round London to get home and I don't want to leave it too late; I've got work in the morning.
>
> *(To audience.)* Which crashes and burns, because

Olivia took the Victoria line to get here and it was 'working just fine'.

[Shit.]

(To table.) Yeah, but I've got this seed of a headache forming and the tube always makes it worse, so if I head off early, I should be able to make it home before it proper kicks off.

Let it settle. Scan their faces to see whether they're buying it. Slight wince for good measure, but nothing too big.

(Beat.) And we're good. I gather my bag, shoot them a sad smile, and I'm almost free and clear until I hear Abby say, 'Look who's too good for us now, eh?'

[Leave it.

Leave it.

Leave i-]

(To table.) ME?!

[Shit.]

I'M the one acting like I'm too good for YOU?

Fine. You want to know why I'm leaving, Abby? I'm leaving because I can't afford this food!

It's all very well for you lot, with your salaried jobs and your benefits and your free gym memberships and your fucking Friday wine evenings at your posh, windowed offices on the billionth floor of some swanky Central London skyscraper. You'll sit down and order a starter and a main and a cocktail, and then three more cocktails, because hey, why not treat yourself? It's a birthday after all!

But I don't have that kind of money. I can barely afford a salad here.

So, let's just imagine I hadn't tried to leave. I stay, everything's cool, I order my shitty little salad while you get the surf and turf, or the oysters, or whatever £35 entrée you decide on. And I'm nibbling on my sad rocket leaf, and at some point, someone will ask me, 'Oh, Danni, aren't you hungry?' And then I have to lie about how full I am even though I'm absolutely starving.

Or you guys order your cocktails or your glasses of wine and then there'll be a, 'Danni, get yourself a drink, come on, we're celebrating!' And then if I don't order one, I'm, like, this big party downer.

Or-or-or, even worse, someone orders champagne for the table.

I hate it when you guys order things for the table. Because no one actually notices that I haven't touched whatever you've decided to share, and I can't bring it up because then it seems like I'm stingy!

I love you guys, which is why I keep putting myself

through this fucking torture to see you. I just don't see why every time we hang out, I have to think about contacting my bank for a small personal loan!

It fucking sucks to be the poor one. Alright? It's not fun. It's not fun having to think of stupid excuses because it's embarrassing to admit I can't pay my own way. It's not fun having to beg my housemates for money before I meet up with you lot. And it's definitely not fun making a knob of myself, yelling at my friends in a fancy restaurant!

Also, I apologise about the 'shitty salad' comment, I'm sure the salads here aren't shitty. I expect they're actually very nice.

Leaves the restaurant.

Tactics
by Sam Butters

Curley Bro, how many times do I have to tell you? My.
System. Works. How many girls do I get weekly?
Daily?! Especially in here, the Hardwick Arms is my
Theatre of Dreams for – Shit! There she is. Katie
fucking Longhurst. Man, no wonder you're basically
in love with her, she's gorgeous. She's a smoker too,
that's well sexy. Might try for it myself. Jokes.
Remember in Year Nine when she stubbed her toe
in the science room and she screamed so loud it
gave you a hard-on for a week? Lol.

Dickhead, do you want my help or not? Right. Face
the bar. Act uninterested. Order twelve shots of
tequila just like George Best did.

Holy – She keeps giving you the old one-two glance.
Don't fucking turn round, bruv! Keep your eyes on
the bar like you don't care, you're just here for the
pints. Get me a Guinness and blackcurrant juice too.

Fuck off, it makes it taste better.

Girls love it too – they say if you have a fruity drink
it means you're okay with your femininity. Which I
totally am. And that's what makes me irresistible.
You should watch RuPaul, mate. Me and Laura
binge it every night and it proper turns her on that I

enjoy watching it. Meant to be watching it tonight but told her I've got shit to do at work. First night out with my boy being single? Ain't missing that for the world.

I know it's been hard since Becky gave you the chop but it's time to get out there again, son.

She was a bit mental anyway. Remember she said that I was a shit mate and there's a special place in hell for people like me? And that you should stop hanging round with me cus I'm a bad influence and Laura is an idiot for being with me? And that I'm well cocky and arrogant? What a binner. I knew she was flirting with me the whole time though. Couldn't help it. So fuck her, mate, it's me and you again! Just like old times. And this girl could be the one, she's gorgeous, she's cute – and her mates are coming back from the smoking area. Okay, shit, it's now or never, mate. We've got to make our move, especially with big Deano eyeing her up in the corner too, fucking Michelin man, you've got no chance, mate, if he gets there first. Okay, chill chill chill.

Ready?

We'll play the old offside trap. Wingman plan 101. Okay, walk with me, mate, just behind me, get ready to break through the line of defence. I'm gonna chat to the bird next to her, leaving you in the clear. Okay, you ready? Go –

Well, aren't you just a piece of – Oh fucking shit, hey baby!

Laura? Oh my fucking God. Hey angel face, what – what are you doing here, baby? It was just so funny actually, me and my bro here were just... I was just... fuck.

The Look
by Sam Liu

ASH is a half-Chinese, half-British 20-year-old from Liverpool.

Ash   You really think I'm that stupid, don't ya?
But the fact of the matter is, Howard, the minute I
got here I put my phone down on that coffee table,
I pressed 'record'. See? Oh… *now* you want me to
leave? You've changed your tune. But I don't think
I'll be goin' just yet – haven't finished me champagne.

Had it all planned out, didn't you? I'd come round
tonight, all big-eyed and bushy-tailed, a little rabbit
caught in your headlights, dazzled by your swanky
apartment an' your bespoke furniture made out of
Mongolian bamboo, or whatever the fuck it was you
said. You'd get me drunk, offer me some coke. And
then what? I'd suck your dick? Bit of a leap, Howard. But I bet you thought it was goin' really well,
didn't ya? Sorry about that. If only I could be as
defenceless as you assumed, maybe your second-
rate Harvey Weinstein tribute act might've worked.
But never mind eh? You live an' learn. I know I
certainly am.

Living.

And learning.

Shall we have a listen back? There's plenty of high-lights: 'You need a big man to fuck you, don't you, you slut?' Charming. Or how about when you called me your 'little Asian twink'? Ooh, and it was 'Little Oriental whore' at one point, wasn't it? Gotta be honest, I haven't heard that one before. I could post this little playlist of Howard's Greatest Hits on Twit-ter right now, an' I might do, if you don't shut up and sit your arse down an' listen to what I've got to say.

Spent me whole life not fittin' in. Always having to make my own way. I'd moved to this city where I can barely afford to eat, an' got a job in some wanky Chinese restaurant where the owner told me no 'ethnic accents' allowed. I felt like sayin' to her: does Scouse count? I was a little half-Chinese queer boy miles from home, who was shit at maths an' loved fashion – what else was I gonna do but start an Instagram? I never thought I'd actually get Insta famous. Me mum thought it was dead stupid. 'You can't pay the leccy bill in Insta likes, Ashley!' she'd say to me.

But she changed her mind when you popped up. You've got that power, ya know? Howard Reeves, I told her, *Howard Reeves*, from one of the flashiest modellin' agencies in London, wants to take on little ol' me! She was bowled over. An' I thought: thank fuck, I've made it, I'm the next Kate Moss. I honestly thought someone was finally givin' me the golden ticket, an' when you told me I was the future of fashion, an' that I had the look that everyone wanted, an' that everyone was so bored of all the same models, all cut from the same cloth – that ethnic was in and Asian was trending, like a fool, I believed ya.

An' do you know what your assistant said to me? She was givin' me the standard 'where are you from?' spiel, an' I told her Liverpool, an' she asked if I spoke Cantonese, an' I told her, no, cos my mum's white & my Chinese dad fucked off a long time ago. An' she said to me, 'Well, Ash, you still might want to... *lean* on your heritage a bit, you know, when people ask, it can play really well'. I just nodded, like, uh-hm, okay. 'And the Liverpudlian side of things,' she says to me, 'accent-wise, maybe we could soften it around the edges a bit?' An' I just went along with it, Howard! Cos I'm used to bendin' myself to what other people expect, what they want. An' because I wanted to be a big fuckin' success, an' be featured in *Vogue,* an' prove all those fuckers wrong who told me I couldn't do it. Just like I went along with it when you asked me round tonight, even though there were little alarm bells goin' off in my head. Only this time, I thought, I want some leverage if it goes tits up. And now it seems, Howard, the tits are up.

You want me to go along with your fucked-up little fantasy, cos-play your idea of some little Eastern submissive? Sorry, love, I'm just not that into you. An' if I don't – then what? I'll never work in this town again? I'll go on the blacklist? I'm quakin'. You an' me are done , Howard, that's for sure, but if you even whisper a word about me try an' get in my way, this gets broadcast to the whole world. And that's a pretty little oriental promise. Ooh, listen to me, I sound like Liam Neeson. And you? You sound like a nobody. Keep it that way, yeah?

I'll be going now, Howard. I've got more meetings in the morning.

Thanks for the champagne.

Cheers.

The Offer
by Daniel Reid-Walters

Dee   So. You – are a lie. Yeah?
Who you are, where you've come from, our friendship, everything. All lies.

(Pause.) You drop that on me, and then straight   after you want to offer me funding for uni? Only it won't be you paying, will it? It'll be your parents. So another lie there then. Do they even know you're doing this, offering their money out? Of course they don't, and they probably don't care, do they?

I mean, that's just typical Chris, so impulsive. Does what he wants. Gets what he wants. The 'free spirit'. Born into a life where you never heard no, and everything's an adventure. I suppose that almost explains all your pretence then really. Nights out where you let me pay for all your drinks, when we had no money for the gas or electric, stealing toilet roll from the fucking uni toilets. All fun and games, just living that real hardcore uni lifestyle, the type of shit you laugh about years after it's over. And you're telling me now, you could have stopped all that. You had – have – the money, to have at least stopped us going cold. And you chose what? To lower yourself to my level for a laugh. Did you go back to your fucking mansion in between terms, and laugh outrageously about it all with your private school chums?

I never thought I'd ever get to rub shoulders with people like you, the superrich. I knew the arts to be a viable career only for those with money. And I fought with myself to choose another dream, take the safe option. But I gained a place. The next challenge was, how do I pay for it. Then I learned a new word: bursary. And I jumped at the chance to be here. Thinking that I wouldn't be the only one getting financial help, there'd be at least one other person who would understand me, and where I'm coming from. I thought you were one of those people.

How wrong I was. *(Beat.)* I wouldn't have judged you, Chris. I actually think I would have been able to get to know you, the real you, and perhaps we could have learned something from each other. *(Pause.)* You took that choice away from me.

And now, when my funding's collapsed, and I'm packing my bags to head back to that council estate, where I'm proud to come from! – you stand there being the generous saviour, offering me another bloody choice. To forget all the lies and take your money, to save my education. *(Pause.)* At this point, that choice isn't mine either. There's no way I can refuse.

(Beat) So it's another yes for Christopher. I'll take the funding, and the chance to continue my training. I'll go on living with you. Still be your housemate. Your scene partner. Your 'bestie'. Even let you go on calling me 'bro'. But the truth is, it'll never be the same.

The Spider
by Aaron Douglas

Jacob   Fuck, I think I'm bleeding. Again.

So, this— *(indicates the carnage)* all of this— wasn't me. Well, okay, it *was* me but technically, it wasn't.

There was a spider, so— I'm absolutely not suggesting the spider pulled the curtains from the railings. I'm not. But the thing is, he *was* on them. I tried to get him and then he fell and I couldn't, for the life of me, find him. I sort of panicked and then to stop myself from falling I grabbed them and – ta-dah!

The coffee table, I will replace. Don't you worry about that. In fact, I was thinking of getting you a new one anyway, actually. A happy accident, I would say. But, yes, the spider *did* crawl on it and I tried punching at it as it scuttled across and wasn't aware of my strength. You should've seen me! Like Hulk but a bit smaller. Less green. More red.

I felt so strong that I was able to move *all* my boxes to the van in less than an hour. Embarrassing doing it in broad daylight though, all the neighbours poking their nosy little beaks around the curtains.

Oh, and you know that urn that you always said you should get rid of? Well, lucky you. That's gone, now. It's in a black bag outside, in pieces...

Grandma is in the Pyrex jug on the side. It was all I could find. I was losing a lot of blood from the— I think I must've cut myself on the pieces of urn. Knocked into it moving the photo albums. Not like she's going to mind. She's lucky! She didn't have to live through this little nightmare, eh? What a fucking public spectacle you've made of all this! We should've invited the whole neighbourhood to watch it all unfold. Fancy buttering some fucking popcorn and delivering it door-to-door; fiver a piece? We'll earn enough to pay for another coffee table! A nice one made of fucking tempered glass. Plonk an IKEA catalogue on it; replace those *horrible* photo albums!
Hmm? That would be good? Wouldn't it? That would be fucking grand!

Beat.

Dad's signed the divorce papers and stuff, but I got blood all over them. So, you might need to order some new ones or something. Might take a while, maybe... I don't know how that all works. You're the divorce expert, I guess.

I caught it though, by the way. The spider.

The Unravelling of Linus Wong
by Stephen Hoo

Linus So that's erm, yeah, that's, so you gave me, and
your order was… so I owe you 70p? No, 30p… to
round it up? To round it up. Yes. No? What? Yo, why
you smilin' for? Oh fuck, wait! Fuck fuck fuck! Sorry
yeah, the till's blown innit.

(Laughing.) Nahhhh I'm just havin a laugh, fam,
AHHHHH!!! I got you, innit. Yeah, I was just joshin
wiv you. My bad my bad. *(Suddenly serious.)* True
say yeah YOU gotta come correct and give ME £1.70
and then transaction's been done – actioned, yeah,
feel me? Can't do one on me. Look at me. I'm a
Chinese bruvah. Maths is my jam, my forte, my fing,
my ting. We invented the abacus. No need for cash
registarrr! Pfft.

Now you're having a laugh. No, you are actually
laughing at me. That's proper mean, bruv. For reals.
I get it. It's my epicanthic Asian eyes. You can't
fathom this moment could arrive and now you're
discombobulated yet humoured. However, this
moment of dread has lingered over me like some
botched Maths GCSE exam for time. The fear of
needing to go back to basics, pre tech, and utilising
the frontal lobe needed for the task at hand. *(Kisses
teeth.)* Where's that bloodclart abacus when you
need it?

Wait a second, though. I know you. You used to go Burns House Pupil Referral unit as well, yeah? Yeah, I remember you. You used to drag me for being shit at maths even though you was worse! 'But you di Chiney man dem,' you used to say. 'Ain't you people good at maths?' 'DJ Maths but the DJ bruk!' No wonder mans is triggered!

Yeah. I can't do numbers. And me being part of the Chinese diaspora has gotten me vexed with the weight of expectation in this moment and you accusin'. I'm bespectacled, tidy looking and my epicanthic folds convey an air of mathematical genius which you know full well I can't fly through.

That's why you came in, isn't it? To order your special fried rice, with that nasty sweet 'n' sour and sesame prawn yuckiness and a side of deepfried cabbage we're gonna call seaweed. Then take advantage of my dyscalculia. Do me over. Don't deny. You can't play a playa, man. Trust!

Softens.

We ain't enemies, fam. We live on the same side of the divide.

You hear that? That's Cardi B playing, ain't no Britpop riffs n ting playing up in this place. RnB, China beats, Ragga, Grime AND K-pop – that's my mixtape... people need to know I got levels. And you see this? *(Referring to himself.)* This is more than 'here's your white people's Chinese food which my dad just bashed out in a wok that ain't never been washed out of respect for my ancestors.' This is authentic, traditional proper pre-Mao cuisine... with a lickle rice and peas and Ogbono soup on the menu. Seen?

Yes Dad, I'm coming!

Suddenly morose.

I got levels.

But I forgive you. For your foolishness, your face-tiness and the division of it all. It's not your fault. The shitstem got us all twist-up and turning on each other when we're basically family.

You know what, just take the food. On the house. Oh yeah, I forgot the free prawn crackers.

No seriously, you don't have to... Okay, okay man. Sweet. Next one's my treat. Laters!

Sighing happily, he looks at the £20.

Hey! This is fake! Oi!!!

Their Life My Lie
by Kadiesha Belgrave

MORGAN – age 18-23, any race. Male or female or non binary.

Morgan   You know, when I used to go to a friend's yard I'd always wonder what their parents thought. They were always nice and polite and shit, but deep down I'd suspect they knew that I was a fraud.

Truth it, when I moved schools for sixth form I wasn't thinking of grades or what their school achieved, I was thinking of the area it was in, almost as if I wanted to eradicate myself completely from the ends. As if being from ends was some type of fucking crime that needed to be concealed. You know none of my friends at sixth form were ever invited to my house. I told 'em I lived on the other side of the river. *(Sniggering as if to hide embarrassment.)* Which I did in a way. I imagined they'd take one look at the place and wince. I would always think about what would make them want to run faster – a large kitchen window with beetle-looking bug things scattering around its windowsill, or that in order to get to my flat we'd have to get in the lift with that crazy woman who screams nonsense at the concierge every morning. Or the autistic boy who hits at you when you get too close and you can't get angry at either of them 'cause we're the unlucky ones... the forgotten. We're the teen mothers, the crackheads, the ones with the anger issues, the ones smoking spliff on the stairwell, the ones that hide the shanks in a safe spot for when the enemy approaches, the ones with no music in the doctor's waiting room.

But people at school wouldn't get that if I explained it to them using an Excel spreadsheet so I'd stay silent… and wonder if their parents were in arrears, or if they'd be on the phone to the council pleading for them to come and fix the FUCKING damp in the corner of my mum's bedroom wall that has been there from day dot…

MORGAN is up and pacing around the room now.

…or if they argue with their parents about something so minor like not being able to make chicken dinosaurs cause the FUCKING oven doesn't work and we can't get that fixed 'cause Mum don't have insurance and we need to save up 'cause the washing machine's been making weird noises again.

And I know what they'll see if they find out I'm lying – you know, about the big family ski trip I have coming up… or the new indoor gym my parents are planning to build in our 4-bedroom house – I know what they'll see. No matter how much money I steal off my dad's debit card or the amount of times I pronounce my T's at the end of words I KNOW what they'll see... They'll see the fraud, the teen mum, the statistic. The truth.

Two Cities
by Paul Bradshaw

CHRIS, 20. Working-class Londoner.

Chris   You know what your problem is, Billy? I do. Your problem is that you don't want to be in our world. You see our world as a place full of stupid people that you can't stand yourself seeming like. You think we're scum. And you think you're better than us. You always have done.

But you're not better than us, Billy.
You're worse.
Because you're exactly like us... 'cept you're ashamed.

You can't see that there's nothing here for the likes of us. Nothing for us to do, no chance of us getting anywhere in life. 'Cause them bastards in power, they don't want us to succeed. They need us to stay poor with no voice, no opportunities. They need us to stay put, keep quiet, stack their shelves, clean their shit up after them and stay in our lane! Well, fuck all of them. And fuck you!

Look around you, you mug! Do you see any of them helping us? Huh? Any of them taking a chance on one of us? They don't want to help us. Has anyone around here managed to make something of themselves? No! The rich get richer and we're stuck here in the gutter with the shit! Fighting to survive. It's like... two cities. Our world and theirs. Us. And Them. It's fucked!

'Course you think 'cause they gave you a scholarship they can't all be bad! But you're wrong. If you can't see that then you're a bigger fool than I thought. Don't let them cunts at that school trick you into thinking there's a place for you in their world or that you can *change*. Because you can't change, Billy.

You'll always be the broke kid from the estate to them. *Always*. The sooner you realise that, the better.

Uniform
by Barbara Williams

TOMMY is a sixteen year-old from the North East of England who has come to tell his favourite teacher that he's joining the army.

Tommy What you lookin' at iz like that for, Miss? Are you gonna try 'n' tell iz what to do 'n' all? Think I'm some braindead, brainwashed, St-George-brandishin' sheep, is that it? Y'kna, there was a time when people respected soldiers. No one's got any respect anymore.

You're just worried I've messed up your results now I dain't need me GCSEs. I thought you were different, but you're all the same. You teachers act like exams are the be all and end all. You tell us no qualifications means no college, no job, no money, trapped. You take wuh on trips to 'broaden our horizons', to try and convince wuh to get up and leave, as if no one would choose to live round here. Well, what if we like it here? There's nowt wrong with bein' proud of where you come from. What kind of message is that for kids like me?

Anyway, you should be pleased: I *am* gettin' out. I *am* gettin' a career. But I'm doin' it on *my* terms. No one forced iz. I can make me own mind up.

And you know what? I thought of you, when they did their little speech, Miss. Cos it was a lovely little alliterative triplet that did it: 'The army will give you determination, drive, and discipline,' they said. Funny word, that – 'discipline'. Me and my mates laugh at discipline. It's never been somethin' that belonged to wuh, but somethin' that was done to wuh. No one ever uses that word positively here. Or if they do they're tellin' wuh it's somethin' we haven't got, somethin' we need. I'm sick of bein' defined by things I haven't got. When are people gonna concentrate on what I have?

They see somethin' in me that none of you lot do. I only did one day of tests and next thing I knew I was in. I mean, you'd think they'd take more care – some of the lads there were off their nuts! 'N', not bein' funny like, but I've seen videos 'n' that from Afghanistan... Some people come back really messed up. I was surprised how quickly it hap-pened...

You know what's weird though, you know what me mam said when I told her? She said, 'Your Granda used to be in the army.' I had no idea. He never, ev-er mentioned it. I felt a bit funny then. It's like you've been marchin' along this path, right, and you thought you were leadin', but then you realise that actually you were followin' all along. Still, better than followin' in me da's footsteps, I suppose, or else I'd end up in friggin' prison.

I had a nightmare, last night. I was marchin' behind me da, chained to him by the ankle. And his da was in front of him, attached to the chain. Miles and miles of the backs of people's heads. It went on forever. Do you believe that, Miss, that your life's mapped out for you?

Here, Miss, are you cryin'?

Voice
by Sam Purkis

Sam   The biggest problem facing the underclass... is politeness. I'm meant to stand here at your out-reach showcase and beg for a bursary whilst show-ing you my authentic self, yeah? Why have you got a dress code then? Fuck your suits. Fuck your ties. This is how I dress. Tracksuit. Chain. Proud. Pomp and pretense leads to flag-nonces and prefects. I'm tired of smiling through gritted teeth whilst you chat bollocks, and not saying that it was your peo-ple and your system that have taken my home. Then moved me out of my city and then, when eve-ry physical and geographical entity of my identity has been snatched, you want my voice.

The voice that can't be heard over the clash of the class war. To the poncy right we are disposable flesh bags useful to protect Queen and Country on the front line, and to the liberal left we're just grunting bigots and war criminals. To both sides less than, to both sides scum. And if you do play ball and become rich, these days you can't speak up on so-cial issues otherwise you are branded a champagne socialist, which although it sounds like a great fuck-ing rap name is another tool to silence. Shut up and fucking play. The ancient ruling elite are now backed by the middle classes, the 'agree with me or we'll tell you to kill yourself on Twitter' classes. The 'we need to tackle obesity and eat more quinoa so we'll ban frozen pizzas whilst happily watching your children starve' classes.

Fuck this. I won't just fit into your angry young man genre, I am young. I am a man and yeah, sometimes I'm pretty fucking angry, but I can love too. But you'll never write about that, will you? We love. We love our parents even when one or more of them abandon us, we love knowledge even when our schools throw us out. Apparently our country needs us... to be uneducated but on time, scared but on the front line, politically passive but ready to commit war crimes, so let's all get dressed to be ready to die on time. My voice is not the same. I don't understand it. I don't want it.

My real voice is roaring, caged inside my head, and some kind of implanted device filters my thoughts every time one tries to leave my skull. Like some once-great symphonic conductor who has lost the faith of his orchestra. The harder he pushes, the farther it drifts away. Aware of the discord every time I open my mouth and it makes me want to become a mute. And so I let them take my voice. Demolishing and gentrifying the beautiful East End pronunciations of the brilliant market salesmen and even better gangsters and boxers I was born into, bartered for the chance to work in a reception on the ground floor of their sky-scraping, phallic piss-monuments. I'm an imposter in my own body, lugging round an instrument I don't know how to play, and with every sound that comes out of it, I hate myself a little bit more. But today this is me. Speaking up.

And saying

Fuck.

You.

Wee Audrey and the Lockjaw Monster
by Lynne Jefferies

Bethan Dinnie you dare tell me to watch my tone, Audrey. You fuckin – You know what, you wanna ken how I got Tara? Because someone kicked the shit oot of her, taped her mouth shut and thew her in the river. I was walking home from work and I saw it. I heard her hit the water, the yelp, the sound of laughter and boots running away. I climbed doon and dragged her by the leg back to the bank. I used my bottle opener from work to tear open the gaffa tape and the first thing she did was lick ma face. It broke my fuckin' heart, so I promised her that I would keep her safe.

The first time someone crossed the road to avoid her I actually enjoyed it. I've never instilled fear in anyone, and she did it just walking. Suddenly we were protecting each other – she didn't trust strange men either. But guess what, Audrey, despite that, she has never so much as growled at anyone. She's pure joy, how can you hate pure joy? I realised we were both working through our trauma together, she was the support I needed to heal. She gave me purpose, she let me laugh again, she... You won't believe me but she made me realise I can love, and um worthy of love.

Now enter you, and your bullshit, who took one look at her and decided you knew *everything* about her. A Pitbull Devil. A lockjaw monster, who will one day no doubt take a bite oot of your precious wee Sebastian. So the meddlin' coppers kicked in ma kitchen door and dragged her away. They put a tape measure to her back to decide whether or not she was dangerous. A fuckin' tape measure. Didney matter she was perfectly behaved. Didney matter she's got certificates in obedience. Fuckin measurements over actions. Millimetres dictated whether she was illegal. But guess what darlin, she's too small. They gave her back to me this morning. If the millimetres decided she was a pitbull she could have been destroyed without me ever seeing her again.

An' you have the audacity to tell me my dug is dangerous? There's nothing more dangerous than you. So you ken what Audrey, you'll be the one paying for that kicked-in door, and you'll be apologising to me and to Tara right fucking now.

When the Fun Stops
by Shakira Newton

Jack   I love your daughter. She's carrying my son. I know
it's hard for you to believe 'cause my actions haven't matched my words, but I don't want this life
for him. I'm trying *so* hard to change.

I've put myself into Gamers Anonymous, I rung up
EE and got 'em to block all the gaming sites from my
phone. I promise, Sue, whether she wants me in her
life or not, I'm gonna do right by your daughter and
my son.

You know I even walk a different way to Tesco now?
Literally just to avoid walking past one of those
places. I can't even stand the sight of 'em anymore.
They're like arcades for pathetic adults who can't
resist the flashing lights and the little stickers.

I hate those stickers – 'when the fun stops, stop' –
How can a tiny yellow sticker emit so much patroni-
sation? Like what are they even on about? 'When
the fun stops' – The fun never fucking started.
People only get sucked into this mess because they
come from nothing.

When you grow up on an estate where the richest
bloke you know only got that way from selling
masses of moody baccy that he and his 'associates'
– his braindead cousins – brought back from Turkey,
you realise very early doors you got two choices for
who you're gonna be in life. You're either a settler

or a hustler. Turns out I'm both. And neither. And I'm not saying any of this as an excuse, alright? Just hear me out.

Four sons and an abusive husband my mother had to feed, clothe and bath using her benefits and Provvy loan. And without any thanks most of the time. Booze eventually killed my dad, and the new alpha of the family, my oldest brother, is too busy feeling sorry for himself and playing video games in his room to step up; so, it's on me. At the age of nineteen I 'ad to be what my dad could never be, and what my mum and brothers never 'ad, and what my bird and soon-to-be nipper needed – and I 'ad to do it quickly.

Now, I didn't get no GCSEs and I di'nt 'av no 'get rich quick' tobacco scheme in my head neither. That's how I ended up 'ere. My fick little head got enticed by the flashing lights and fairground sounds of the bookies. Started off one or two bets 'ere and there, y'know, off to the casino after a night out. But before long I've got ten fake accounts for twenny different betting sites and I'm slipping my hand into Mum's purse for her debit card whilst she sleeps at night to make more. And before you judge me and butt in like you always do, I already fucking know, alright?!

It was never a lot. Ten, fifteen quid maybe. And I'd never do it again.

Imitates looking at phone watching the money roll in as he bets, reacting to each number accordingly.

> Fifteen pound
> Thirty-five
> Fifty!
> Twenty-five
> Two pound... shit
> Fifteen
> Twenny
> Seventy!
> ... Five
> Zero.

Stops imitating, begins to speak to mother-in-law again.

> Minus two hundred.
> Minus fifteen thousand.
> Minus a credit score.
> Minus a missus and a kid.
> Minus a family to rely on.
> Minus a will to live.

> So, yeah, they put these stickers on the machines to ease their consciences, knowing full well they're sending people to squalor. To their graves. And the most fucked up thing about it all? After everything it's done to me, all the ways it's torn me and my family apart... Even though I know exactly what they're doing – I still can't stop. But I *am* trying.

Wrecked
by Timotei Cobeanu

Sheffield City Centre.

Chloe   Rehab, 10 a.m. First day out. It's one of them cloudy days today. But it's alright. I'm off to my first interview in months cos my life is finally getting sorted the fuck out.

N16 to Sheffield, National Express. Crying babies, fed up parents. I almost lost it, though. When they won't stop kicking the back of your seat, screaming for food, or the fella in front of you lowers their seat onto you as if they're some politician getting a blowjob in the back of a limo. Can you not, Bobby? Ta. Jesus. And the bleeding smells! All that semi-digested Subway on top of unwashed feet. Shit. It turns 12.

Bus running late.

Get off, relieved. Still time. Start walking to this address that the woman in the rehab gave me when I left. I'm pretty chuffed. Lost, but chuffed. It's not far or owt, but it's pretty chocka let me tell you. So I go to myself, I'll just ask someone direct an' we'll be alright. Nice fucking one. Everyone in town centre getting absolutely trashed. Tripping over buzzing Tramlines. Wreckin' their heads like cracked-up pigeons. Chewin' their gums like basic morons. Like me in my last year of college. What was I thinkin' asking for directions? These lot can barely walk and talk let alone know what a fucking Job Centre is or where it might be hiding. Hell's version of Heaven on Earth it is, I tell ya. Little daredevils at every corner shop, sporting their sparkles; glittery hipsters with silvery eyes an' puffy pink scarves bought from Primark, lightin' up their Sterlings like they was Cuban cigars. Yeah, I'm a tad jealous inside. Secretly luvin' their gritty teen partying. But I'm going to a fucking job interview so I'm focused and raging. Jealous but not tempted.

State of this lot.

This ain't Las Vegas love, this is Dev Green, so stop acting like an extra in *Boogie Nights* or summat! Scally-chuffin-wags!

So I keep going, pushed and pranked and joked at, youths throwin' up on me shoes, getting cat-called by cunts stinkinga cheap booze, sweaty skins making friction like pigs packed in pens. I'm 'avin' a right laugh. Round the corner a cheeky pair of laddies snorting a baggie of MD be'ind a carousel where children play. And above all, a right big policeman ridin' a massive fuck off gee-gee as if it were World War 2 or summat! G E SUS. And it's only 12 A.M. ON A FRIDAY.

Anyway. Can't waste a minute longer now. Got to look my best, be my best today. It's gonna be alright, I hope. Cos my life... my life needs sortin' out.

You and Me, Stinky-Arse
by Deanna Arthur

Lucie Okay. Okay. Shhhh. I'm sorry I shouted. It's not your fault, and I do try to keep that in mind.

I'd never be saying this if I thought you'd take it to heart and need a posh wanky therapist in years to come.

I just

Think back to before you: who I was and who I was going to be and I... You know I was going to be a superstar? Yep! Your mum! I was going to get a scholarship to a fancy American college, and then I was going to get picked up and signed in LA and I was going to sing all over the world. And then I did a stupid stupid thing. And here we are!

God, what a terrible mum. I wouldn't trade you for the world and I hope you always know that. It's not even resentment – and I'm not just thinking for me now: for you, I mean. As you get older and figure out that your dad couldn't be arsed and left you, left your mum, didn't even respect us enough to help. How am I supposed to explain that to you?

I think I'm scared for you already, that's what it is. I don't want there to come a time when you, naturally, want more than just me. And you go looking and you're hopeful and then you see him for what he is and can't stand all the things about him that I couldn't stand, and hate him. Even worse, you might bond, think he's great, wonder why I've been hiding him from you all this time and then hate me. Fuck. I guess you're going to need a posh wanky therapist either way, aren't you?

I couldn't ever hate you, I'm sorry I – for all that. I hate... this. I hate all the things I can't give you. And yeah, to be honest, I do, I hate all the things I can't give myself too.

What I really fucking hate

Is the fact that some people can get on with their life, knowing that someone as beautiful as you is in the world. Ready for them to love, their baby. Someone as gorgeous, and super smart and happy as you. And he just doesn't want to know. That's what I hate. I need help and I don't even want to ask him and he's just told me he can give me £20 for the month 'cause he's just lost a job. Do you know what we can spend that on? Nappies. Fucking nappies. God, we've got to laugh, haven't we, or we'll cry. We'll do alright, though, we've just got to figure out how to make it work, haven't we.

Maybe we'll both need a posh wanky therapist. Maybe it's a good thing and we'll make him pay for it! Yay! Yes, we will! Ooh, okay, stinky arse, let's get you changed, shall we?